Powers of Time

A Univocal Book

Drew Burk, Consulting Editor

Univocal Publishing was founded by Jason Wagner and Drew Burk as an independent publishing house specializing in artisanal editions and translations of texts spanning the areas of cultural theory, media archeology, continental philosophy, aesthetics, anthropology, and more. In May 2017, Univocal ceased operations as an independent publishing house and became a series with its publishing partner the University of Minnesota Press.

Univocal authors include:

Miguel Abensour
Judith Balso
Jean Baudrillard
Philippe Beck
Simon Critchley
Fernand Deligny
Jacques Derrida
Vinciane Despret
Georges Didi-Huberman
Jean Epstein
Vilém Flusser
Barbara Glowczewski
Évelyne Grossman
Félix Guattari
David Lapoujade
François Laruelle

David Link
Sylvère Lotringer
Jean Malaurie
Michael Marder
Quentin Meillassoux
Friedrich Nietzsche
Peter Pál Pelbart
Jacques Rancière
Lionel Ruffel
Michel Serres
Gilbert Simondon
Étienne Souriau
Isabelle Stengers
Eugene Thacker
Siegfried Zielinski

Powers of Time

VERSIONS OF BERGSON

◇◇◇◇◇◇◇◇◇◇◇◇◇◇◇◇◇◇◇◇◇◇◇◇◇◇◇◇◇◇◇

David Lapoujade

Translated by Andrew Goffey

A Univocal Book

University of Minnesota Press
Minneapolis
London

The University of Minnesota Press acknowledges the contribution of Jason Wagner, Univocal's publisher, in making this volume possible.

Originally published in French as *Puissances du temps,* copyright 2010 by Les Éditions de Minuit

Published by the University of Minnesota Press
111 Third Avenue South, Suite 290
Minneapolis, MN 55401-2520
http://www.upress.umn.edu

Printed in the United States of America on acid-free paper

The University of Minnesota is an equal-opportunity educator and employer.

23 22 21 20 19 18   10 9 8 7 6 5 4 3 2 1

Library of Congress Cataloging-in-Publication Data
Names: Lapoujade, David, author.
Title: Powers of time : versions of Bergson / David Lapoujade ; translated by Andrew Goffey.
Other titles: Puissances du temps. English
Description: Minneapolis : University of Minnesota Press, 2018.
| Series: Univocal | "A Univocal book." | Includes bibliographical references.
Identifiers: LCCN 2017059141 (print) | ISBN 978-1-5179-0427-2 (pb)
Subjects: LCSH: Bergson, Henri, 1859–1941. | Time.
Classification: LCC B2430.B43 L27313 2018 (print) |DDC 194–dc23
LC record available at https://lccn.loc.gov/2017059141

Contents

Introduction
Time and Affect

To say nothing of the kind of person who would insist that our "intuition" was instinct or feeling. Not one line of what I have written could lend itself to such an interpretation.
—*Bergson*

We know that to grasp duration, Bergson's famous duration, it is necessary to feel it flowing in us. According to one of Bergson's examples, the succession of chimes of a bell is first a series of sounds that moves us confusedly before it is a definite number that one can represent distinctly. The "immediate givens of consciousness" are above all emotions; they are the effect that the flowing of time produces on sensibility. But what type of emotion is it a matter of? Doubtless the chimes of the bell have a particular emotional tonality—joyful tocsin, dismal reminder of the time, etc.—but for Bergson this is only a matter of superficial emotions, which belong to the world of representation. More profoundly, there is an emotion that derives from the passage of time itself, from the fact of feeling time flow in us and of "vibrating internally." It is duration itself that is emotion in us. Inversely, it is only through the emotions that we are beings who endure, or rather that we stop considering ourselves as beings so as to become durations, like a sound, which exists or endures through its vibration, and nothing else. In depth, we aren't "beings" any longer but vibrations, resonance effects, "tonalities" at different levels. And the universe itself comes to be dematerialized, to become

1

duration, a plurality of rhythms of duration that are also arranged in depth according to distinct levels of tension.

If we have to turn away from this aspect, it is because on the surface, thinking by concepts—understanding or intelligence—has never managed to grasp the flowing of time, duration properly so called. This critique of intelligence is one of the best known aspects of Bergson's thought. Since Zeno and the beginnings of metaphysics, the intelligence only succeeds in thinking time at the cost of various denaturings; it fragments time, divides it, measures it, reconstructs it, but each time it lets what constitutes its very substance escape. It is in this sense that there are two aspects to experience in Bergson: the aspect of intelligence, a vast, surface plane where everything unfolds horizontally in space, according to the logic of representation, and the aspect of intuition or profound emotion, a vertical world where everything is organized in depth, according to a plurality of levels, sometimes inferior and sometimes superior to that of the intelligence, but always parallel to it, operating according to a time and logic of a different nature.

The intelligence certainly represents a prodigious breakthrough, which extends unceasingly in every direction, but it always remains on the same plane populated with partial visions and recomposed wholes, "objects" and "subjects" that condition and determine each other reciprocally. To the extent that the intelligence is a faculty that is only actualized in humans, this plane also appears as the properly anthropological plane.[1] It is the plane on which we are "human," nothing but human. To ask what happens on this plane—how thinking, affect, knowledge, morality, and so on—proceed on this plane is to rediscover the general question that Hume and Kant already posed in their own way: what is human nature? What is man? Consequently it is not surprising that it is above all the responses of the empiricists and of Kant that occupy this plane: if Bergson never stops criticizing them, then this is as a function of what happens on the other levels, those that escape the intelligence and ensure philosophy merges with "an effort to go beyond the human state."[2]

But passing over to the aspect of intuition or emotion does not mean that one relies on the emotions that the passage of time produces in us. People are sometimes astonished that Bergson said nothing, or almost nothing, about hope, regret, mourning, melancholy—about all those affects that give us access to time. How does it happen that in effect time (or duration) in Bergson is never described as starting from the emotions that it engenders? How is one to explain that time is not described in its most reparative or destructive aspects? Doesn't that even constitute a serious objection against Bergsonism? We are dealing with a duration where one regrets nothing, where one suffers no loss, where one experiences no mourning, where one doesn't stop forging ahead, following the rhythm of unpredictable novelty proper to the élan vital. . . . Bergsonian duration makes nothing disappear. It is the complete opposite of Proustian time, for example, which makes faces collapse and debilitates the spirits, makes beings die as well as the selves that loved them. Should one not agree with Heidegger when he reproaches Bergson for having ignored the irrevocable character of the past?[3]

What would Bergson's response to such objections be? A first response consists in saying that it is a matter of affects that are produced in time and that in this sense they already suppose its existence. Better still, Bergson specifies precisely that one can only attain "completely pure" duration by an effort that is independent of all definite emotion. "There is no doubt but that for us time is at first identical with the continuity of our inner life. What is this continuity? That of a flow or a passage [. . .], flow not implying a thing that flows and the passing not presupposing states through which we pass."[4] Thus, when one listens to a melody, one has to close one's eyes and think just about the melody—but on condition, Bergson specifies, that one erases the difference between the sounds and abolishes the distinctive characteristics of the sound itself, so as to retain only "the continuation of what precedes into what follows and the uninterrupted transition, multiplicity without divisibility and succession without separation, in order finally to rediscover basic time."[5] One must manage to think the flowing independently of the things that flow, like one must think change "in no way attached to a 'thing' which changes."[6] That is when duration, the purely spiritual element of time, its very substance, is set free. It is a matter of a properly Bergsonian reduction, grasping duration and change in themselves, independently of everything that endures and of everything that changes. From this point of view, the temporal affects constitute instead the impure elements that trouble the perception of pure duration, as do the emotions that a melody suggests.

Except one is only considering empirical affects or intratemporal manifestations here. Regret is produced in time and regrets something that occurred in time, at a determinate moment. Can one not conceive a regret or nostalgia of a different order, like a disposition with regard to time in its entirety, in the manner of "transcendental" or "existential" affects able to constitute time in us? So, for example, who better than the melancholic can perceive the irrevocable character of the passage of time? Doesn't time as a whole collapse into the past a priori? Isn't time as a whole always already past for him? Whether one thinks of the young melancholic of Kierkergaard's *Repetition* or the melancholic utterances analyzed by Henri Maldiney, the disposition is always the same: everything is already finished; it is always already too late.[7] "Too late" becomes the a priori structure of all temporalization. As Kierkegaard says on the subject of the melancholic young lover who pines after his true love: "From the first days, he was able to recollect his love. He was essentially through with the entire relationship. In beginning it, he took such a tremendous step that he leaped over life. [. . .] His mistake was incurable, and his mistake was that he stood at the end instead of at the beginning, but such a mistake is and remains a person's downfall."[8]

In the same way, waiting is defined first as an affect that is produced in time. Following Bergson's celebrated example, one must wait for the sugar to melt. . . . Like regret, waiting is open onto other durations—those, precisely, that make us wait, here the very duration of the material universe during which the sugar melts. However, once again, doesn't it turn out that waiting ceases to be in time so as to become a disposition with regard to time in its entirety? Is not living to wait indefinitely for time to pass or for life to begin? One might think of the fate of the character in the Henry James novella *The Beast in the Jungle* whose existence is devoted in its entirety to waiting for something to happen, to being on the lookout like a hunter for the event that will transfigure his existence—life become pure eschatology. All of time is ordered around the event that must happen/ arrive but that never happens/arrives, as if it was precisely waiting that prevented whatever it may be from happening.[9] It is the moral of all the great stories about waiting, from James to Beckett: nothing ever happens to those who wait—nothing other than the fact of having waited in vain. One waits like one regrets: in vain. Waiting is only ever an inverted melancholy, another figure of man's unhappiness. This doesn't prevent the new order of time from being constituted in both cases by an affect or complex of affects.

But how can one not see that if ordinary affects are in time, these others are imprisoned in a sort of outside of time? In one case as in the other, time doesn't pass, or it passes abstractly, outside, as if it no longer concerned them, whereas they live imprisoned in regret or expectation. The course of time is submitted to an imperious order that deprives them of any present. "A present that has already happened, where what has been done keeps on being added, indefinitely, to what has been done, because nothing happens, because there is no event [. . .] there is nothing *new*."[10] But those who

(margin annotations: "concerned with death, judgment"; "address with obvious cause")

5

live exclusively in the present do not grasp the passage of time either as they reduce the two other dimensions of time to the punctuality of the now, the succession of incessant imperatives, with no perspective for them to open up the horizon, in a state of permanent urgency.[11] In every case, time is only ever an external frame that affects or no longer affects those who are imprisoned in that way; that is also why nothing ever happens to them. They are closed subjectivities, imprisoned within their destiny: "One day, the melancholic made up his mind. Straightaway everything is accomplished: destiny engulfs freedom. The unintentional and timeless necessity of destiny is substituted for the temporal irreversibility of the act which can only be ruptured, even in a history, by another free act."[12] They are imprisoned in an outside of time, void of any event and any affect, where nothing occurs and nothing can occur, as if only descending back down into time could return to them both their reality and their freedom.

Haven't these descriptions distanced us from Bergson? And aren't the questions that they raise rather foreign to his thinking? But isn't the contrary the case? Doesn't the displacement that they bring about perhaps lead us back to the very heart of Bergsonism? Is it not in fact Bergson who, from his first book, establishes a relationship between duration and freedom that will be revealed to be indissoluble? The new concept of duration is not only destined to resolve a theoretical problem that the partisans of freewill and determinism do not manage to pose; it is duration that effectively makes us free. It is only in and by duration that one experiences its freedom, just as one ceases to be free when one lives in submission to logics without temporality, like that of melancholy. Similarly, it is by insertion into duration that one makes the "fundamental self" live again, the self that is moved, that "vibrates internally" as if only duration could give us back a life rich in affects. One has the impression that the event that James's character awaits indefinitely—which ends up happening too late, the event through which duration, life, freedom are given back—is what inaugurates Bergsonism.

One can judge this by the description that Bergson gives of the free act: "We will grant to determinism that we often resign our freedom in more serious circumstances [. . .] when our whole personality ought to vibrate. When our most trustworthy friends agree in advising us to take some important step, the sentiments which they utter with so much insistence lodge on the surface of our ego and there get solidified. [. . .] Little by little they will form a thick crust which will cover up our own sentiments. [. . .] But then, at the very minute when the act is going to be performed, something may revolt against it. It is the deep-seated self rushing up to the surface. It is the outer crust bursting, suddenly giving way to an irresistible thrust [. . .] the action which has been performed does not then express some superficial idea, almost external to ourselves, distinct and easy to express: it agrees with the whole of our most intimate feelings, thoughts and aspirations, with that particular conception of life which is the equivalent of all our past experience."[13] If, as Heidegger thinks, there is no sense of irrevocability in Bergson, then this may be because he reverses its destiny so as to substitute for it a sense of vocation. This is what a posteriori explanations testify to: I was made for that. Everything conspired toward this free act that expresses me in my entirety.

If the future opens up once again, then it is on the basis of the deepest past, the past in its entirety, in the style of Proustian time regained—unless it is Proust who is Bergsonian on this point: "Thus all my life up to that day might have been or might not have been summed up under the title: 'A vocation?' In one sense, literature had played no active part in my life. But, in another, my life, the memories of its sorrows, of its joys, had been forming a reserve like albumen in the ovule of a plant. It is from this that the plant draws its nourishment in order to transform itself into seed at a time when one does not yet know that the embryo of the plant is developing though chemical phenomena and secret but very active respirations are taking place in it."[14] Does one not rediscover Bergson's two selves here, the surface self, who lives "in the midst of frivolous amusements, in idleness, in tenderness and in pain," and the self of the depths, who secretly stores up the materials of the literary work to come, "as the seed has in reserve all the ingredients which will nourish the plant"?[15] Isn't it the past, regained in its entirety, that is liberated in the free act of the work to come?

◇◇◇◇◇◇◇◇◇◇◇◇◇◇◇◇◇◇◇

A second question then poses itself, the inverse of the previous question: if, as Bergson says, "the deeper psychic states, those which are translated by free acts, express and sum up the whole of our past history,"[16] then how does one really leave the past? Doesn't one remain in submission to the idea of destiny? Can one conceive a sense of the future that is irreducible to any past? From where does it draw its supposed unforeseeable novelty if it comes from and is explained by the past? Furthermore, in Bergson, isn't it the past that gives its foundation to time in its entirety, if at one and the same time it explains both the present and the future? How, then, does one not read Bergson according to Deleuze's remarks? Deleuze writes, "We say of successive presents which express a destiny that they always play out the same thing, the same story, but at different levels: here more or less relaxed, there more or less contracted. That is why destiny accords so badly with determinism but so well with freedom: freedom lies in choosing the levels. The succession of present presents is only the manifestation of something more profound—namely, the manner in which each continues the whole life, but at a different level or degree to the preceding, since all levels and degrees coexist and present themselves for our choice on the basis of a past which was never present. [. . .] Each chooses his pitch or his tone, perhaps even his lyrics, but the tune remains the same, and underneath all the lyrics the same tra-la-la, in all possible tones and pitches."[17] A melancholic Bergson?

This objection is more serious because it is certainly less external to Bergsonism than the previous objection. Certainly Deleuze does not ignore the importance of the future or the production of the new in Bergson, but he explains them by the way in which each time the past—present in its entirety at each moment of our life—presents different aspects of itself so as to illuminate a situation—which is itself always original and new—with new sense. One understands that in effect our past always presents itself differently on every occasion, as similar as these occasions might be to one another, to the extent that it is the totality of our past that repeats itself each time, but by ceaselessly displacing, condensing, stirring itself up. Doesn't Deleuze find a confirmation of all this in the fact that Bergson substitutes a fundamental self for the surface self, whereas a philosophy genuinely turned toward the future has to go as far as destroying the very form of the self? "As for the third time in which the future appears, this signifies that the event and the act possess a secret coherence which excludes that of the self [. . .] smash[ing] it to pieces, as though the bearer of the new world were carried away and dispersed by the shock of the multiplicity to which it gives birth."[18] Isn't it precisely this third time, the time of the future, that is missing in Bergson's philosophy?

Doubtless one may be led to such a conclusion if one only reads *Matter and Memory*, where, in the final analysis, Bergson only explores two dimensions of time, the present and the past and accounts for the future by the incessantly repeated, always different encounter of the one with the other. Perhaps one might change one's point of view with *Creative Evolution*, where the sense of the future is now explained by the élan vital.[19] But isn't the élan vital in turn defined as an immense, prodigious memory coextensive with all forms of life? Is it not also the incessantly repeated encounter between a matter and a memory? Even supposing that the élan vital designates the manner in which the future attracts us toward it, in which we are oriented toward the future rather than toward the past, how is one not to suppose that the sense of the future is given with the élan vital rather than engendered by it? Doesn't the élan vital figure as a deus ex machina? And there will, in the *Time and Freewill*, indeed be a God to account for all creation.

If the future in Bergson is only understood on the basis of the past, can one still say that Deleuze's reading is correct? One can certainly maintain the hypothesis according to which freedom consists in actualizing the virtualities contained in an élan vital conceived as a memory. But one must then take care not to confuse the two conceptions of the virtual in Bergson. The first defines the past as never having been present; it is always already the old present that it has been, the image in the past of the passing present. The past is a parallel world to that of the present; it is not behind us but alongside us. Thus the past does not have to become past; it is so from the outset. It borders our present life and is formed at the same time as it—not just after the present has ceased to be but at the same time, like a mirror image. Bergson explains clearly that this "memory of the present" is perfectly useless. What use could such an image have, given that we have the original at our disposal? It is a passive, inactive memory that merely gathers up memories automatically as our life unfolds.[20] If it constitutes a reserve, it is only ever a reserve of *sense*.[21] These memories only become useful for a present that is different from those they have been, and it is then that the past usefully clarifies the present, precisely by giving it a sense.

The second definition characterizes the virtual as reserve or potential, as an ensemble of indeterminate, mutely active potentialities, already acting as a multiplicity of tendencies still implicated in one another. Memory is no longer a reserve of sense but of "spiritual energy." The virtual testifies to another form of memory, an active memory informed by life. Deleuze does not confuse the two forms because he distinguishes an ontological memory, a memory of the past in itself, a pure, virtual, impassive, inactive, and useless memory, as well as a psychological, "incarnate" memory that makes this past serve its ends.[22] From ontology to psychology, one passes from one virtual to another, from an inactive virtual to an active virtual, already a power, from a virtual in itself to a virtual for us, thereby converted into a reserve of future that is actualized according to determinate processes. But what is the miracle by which this passage occurs in Deleuze?

One can indeed say that it is the demands of the present, with its incessant succession of imperatives, that makes us actualize such and such a virtuality, but how is it with freedom, which is irreducible to this type of causality? How could freedom find its reason for being by obeying the demands of these imperatives? Must one suppose that by introducing an interval of time between action and reaction, between cause and effect, between imperative and response, by introducing the duration of a hesitation, we introduce into the world a certain portion of freedom?[23] Isn't this difference of rhythm freedom itself? One can indeed see what that signifies for living things, even at the most elementary level: nutrition is what allows the living thing to insert indetermination into the world, to work loose the weft of universal determinism, to introduce a new rhythm of duration into it, but precisely because it has at its disposal a certain reserve of energy to do so.[24]

At another level, from where does the individual draw its power to rupture the weft of the material, social determinism to which it is subjected? We come back to the same point: from where does it draw its "spiritual energy"? What has accumulated in it to the point that it explodes in a free act? What has it nourished itself on? Is it sense, or rather, the multiple significations that our memory has accumulated throughout our lives? That would explain in part the lengthy labor of intuition that Bergson talks about on several occasions, the lengthy duration that it calls for.[25] It is most certainly necessary for any creative act, with its explosive charge. "The work produced may be original and vigorous; in many cases human thought will be enriched by it. Yet this will be but an increase of that year's income."[26] It will only be the recomposition or complexification of a simplicity that escapes it because it is situated on another plane. One can certainly invoke life, the élan vital itself, but that is to rely on the same deus ex machina.

Yet this spiritual energy really must come from memory because everything comes from memory in Bergson, except that it cannot be explained by the two forms of memory that make up perception in *Matter and Memory*. In effect, it cannot be explained by the contraction-memory that contracts the innumerable vibrations of matter and condenses them into qualities, which is what ensures that the present is already a synthesis of the past and that in reality we only perceive the past.[27] Nor can it be explained by the recollection-memory that is only the reserve, inactive in itself, of the whole of our past life, and through which the present receives its signification.[28] As a consequence, one must introduce another form of memory. It is no longer a matter of a memory of the present (contraction) or of a memory of the past (recollection). It is a matter of a memory of the future, for the future.

Parallel to the past that is always already past of recollection-memory, parallel to the incessant becoming present of contraction-memory, there is in the depths still another present that does not pass—and that doesn't stop growing because it accumulates energy, this energy that Bergson calls "spiritual" and that is still so difficult to understand. It is a spirit-memory. It is not the memory of what we perceive in the present; it is not the memory of what we have been. Rather, it is the memory of what we are and what we have never stopped being, even if we have no knowledge of it. It is what provides the figure for time, which opens or closes the future. Its presence, sometimes even its insistence, is explained because there is something in the past— and thus also in the present—that, in a certain manner,

12

has not been lived. Except here there is no relationship with the manner in which recollection is immediately presented in a past that has itself never been lived either—a pure virtual of no use to the present of which it is the already faded image. No, it is a matter here of something that has been present, that has been sensed, but that has not been acted, something that thus keeps itself in reserve, a little like plants accumulate energy that will later be of use to animals.

It is indeed toward life that one must turn, toward what makes of us living beings—or rather toward what makes us feel that we are living beings. It is not a matter of turning toward the élan vital in general but toward the process that made its actualization possible, that is to say, the division of the élan vital into vegetable and animal. This scission was the condition itself of its growth.[29] On the one hand, plants accumulate energy; on the other, animals expend it in movement. Does one not rediscover here the scission that Bergson starts out from in *Time and Freewill*, between the fundamental self and the surface self? Something rises up from the depths and bursts through the surface of the surface self. The entire duration of a life compressed in the frame of an ordinary life is finally liberated and is expressed through one or a series of free acts. On the one hand, emotion accumulates in the depths of the self; on the other, it explodes in a free act. Is it not emotion that constitutes the spiritual energy of a purely intensive spirit-memory, irreducible to recollection-memory and its virtualities? If the future has a sense and if it can be engendered, then it is on the basis of emotion and of emotion alone. Now we have come back to where we started: affect.

But once again, what emotion is it a matter of? As it cannot be either in time or outside of time, what is the nature of the emotion that Bergson makes proper to duration? And what does it turn out to be inseparable from but our freedom? It can only be understood if one conceives and experiences duration as itself inseparable from movement, from the universal "mobility at the base of things."[30] Duration is always the duration of a movement. In the same way, there is only emotion of movement.[31] If in any case Bergson prefers the term "emotion" to "affect," it is doubtless because its etymology already suggests movement. Emotion is the movement by which the spirit grasps the movement of things, of beings, and of itself. Or rather, movement is spirit itself of things and of beings, and it is that from which we "vibrate internally," in depth. In other words, emotion is the virtual movement—that is nonetheless real—of the actual movements that are accomplished in the world.

This is what the fundamental self—the free acts of which are its subsequent expression—doesn't stop filling itself with. What is lacking in the lives we evoked previously? One might say that they lack reality, freedom, and vitality, but first and above all else, they lack the movements that would make them freer, more real, and more lively; they are deprived of the élan vital that would free them from their destiny—or rather, they bend back each nascent movement toward this very destiny. Inversely, to be moved by "pure duration" supposes that one frees oneself from this imprisonment, that one sympathizes with other durations, that one "enter into what is being done," that it "follow the moving reality, adopt the becoming which is the life of things."[32] It is in this sense that Bergson can say that "whatever may be the inner essence of what is or what is done, we are of that essence."[33] We participate in movement in the making insofar as we are moved by it. It is because emotion is not an affect that reacts to the presence or absence of something, which is what is proper to all the so-called temporal affects. It is an affect that is moved by the passage of time or the movement of beings as such. This affect is the emotion of the passage of time itself rather than the moving of beings (or nothings) that populate (or depopulate) it.

Thinking the passage of time, sympathizing with this passage, is precisely to free oneself up from what is, from what attaches us to beings or to nothings. Correlatively, it is the reason why one would search in vain in Bergson for a definition of the past as what no longer *is*, or of the future as what *is* not yet, even though he sometimes expresses himself in this way. Being and nothingness do not allow time to be thought adequately. The whole problem here comes from the fact that thought is fixed to beings rather than to the movement of these beings. Is that not the case with melancholics, who remain fixed on the past or the future? Is it not also properly metaphysical to remain fixed to what was or to what might be, and thus to generate a whole series of false problems? [34] One only becomes a metaphysician or religious by dint of exiting the immanence of duration. If there is no dialectic of presence and absence in Bergson, it is because duration is not attached to being—or to beings. On the contrary, it merges with pure becoming. The emotion of duration is an affect that is no longer an attachment. This is why it is not irrelevant that Bergson discovers duration at the same time as a new conception of freedom. To become attached to duration liberates us from attachment to beings and to nothings to the exact extent that it makes us sympathize with their movements. Bergsonian duration is an ascesis, almost a lesson in morality.

Emotion, sympathy, and attachment thus constitute three aspects of a thinking of affect in Bergson. How, then, is one not to see that the entirety of these questions leads us to set out the portrait of another Bergson? On the basis of concepts that are apparently secondary and sometimes neglected by commentaries, such as the concept of "obscure number" or that of "attachment to life," and indeed even that of "sympathy," other versions of Bergsonism appear: a mathematical Bergson, a perspectivist Bergson, or even a Bergson who is a doctor of civilization. Most often these terms have only been perceived as concessions made to pedagogy or to elegance, but not as concepts in their own right. But this is nevertheless how one must try to consider them, not for reasons of provocation or heresy, but because they are necessary to another understanding of Bergson's oeuvre: they are what enable an indissoluble relationship to be knotted together between time and affect.

The Obscure Number
of Duration

Bergson the
Mathematician

How is the link between the immediate givens of consciousness and the problem of freedom in the first of Bergson's books to be understood? Is it a matter, as the foreword suggests, of a relation of application? Was the problem of freedom "chosen" as one problem among many so as to valorize the fecundity of a new distinction between time and space? With his distinction between two types of multiplicity, the quantitative multiplicities of juxtaposition in space and the qualitative, interpenetrating multiplicities in time, doesn't Bergson sense that he already has a new method, which allows problems to be posed differently, to henceforth be posed "as a function of time rather than space,"[1] at his disposal? And quickly it is effectively not only the problem of freedom but also those of the mind–body relation, the subject/object couple, of matter and of life, and so on, that will make Bergson's work grow in numerous directions.

But did Bergson really have a choice? Isn't it also true that each time a new problem is encountered, freedom returns, always on the same side of the distinction, always on the side of the "immediate givens of consciousness," of the qualitative multiplicities of duration, of the growing tensions of consciousness, of the powers of life and the aspirations of open morality? That would mean that the "immediate givens of consciousness" do not lead to the problem of freedom but that

17

they constitute the very givens of this freedom. It would be less a matter of a relation of application, as Bergson says, than of profound affinities between the two. If this hypothesis is well founded, it supposes that one can manage to distinguish the givens constitutive of this freedom at the heart of the qualitative multiplicities. In what way is the fact of hearing the hour sounding on a nearby clock in a direct relationship with our freedom? In what way are the examples, presented by Bergson as so many "musical phrases" of pure duration, also and inseparably the genetic source of free acts? Perhaps answering this question will allow the descriptions of the free act in Bergson to be better understood; otherwise they seem to spring up miraculously from the depths of consciousness. One can only understand *Time and Freewill* if one tries to respond to these questions—that is to say, if one tries to grasp the profound, indissoluble link between the immediate givens of consciousness and free acts.

◇◇◇◇◇◇◇◇◇◇◇◇◇◇◇◇◇◇◇

What are the immediate givens of consciousness? We know that in *Time and Freewill*, Bergson distinguishes between two types of multiplicity: the numerical, homogenous, distinct, and discrete multiplicities of juxtaposition (which are presented in space), and the qualitative, heterogeneous, confused, and continuous multiplicities of penetration (which are presented in time). Each corresponds to an aspect of the self—the surface self for the former, the fundamental self for the latter. These two selves each represent a point of view of consciousness on itself. We also know that only the qualitative, internal multiplicities, those that perceive the fundamental self, constitute the "immediate givens of consciousness." They cannot appear to the surface self for the simple reason that this latter can only represent multiplicities in a space; its givens are always mediate, symbolic. The surface self is only the self of the mediate givens of consciousness.

The surface self is characterized above all by its symbolic activity of representation: it represents, through the mediation of space, what is presented immediately in time. This signifies that it transforms the immediate givens of consciousness into representations, which are so many active syntheses. The representation of a homogeneous space effectively presupposes an "effort of the intelligence."[2] In this sense the surface self is analogous to the Kantian subject, which must re-present the diversity that is first presented to intuition. Kant thinks in spatial terms; he is the thinker of representation par excellence. Throughout the descriptions of the activity of counting, one can find the syntheses of the Kantian subject without any difficulty, with this difference: they are no longer subject to the formal condition of time but rather to that of space. The apprehension of unity (simple intuition), reproduction of unity in the imagination (distinction and juxtaposition), and summation are the operations by which the self represents to itself a multiplicity in space.[3] Certainly one can object that to count is to count moments in duration, "but the question is whether we have not counted moments of duration by means of points in space."[4] Time is no longer the condition of active syntheses—or rather, it is space that becomes the condition of time proper to the syntheses of the surface self. As in Kant, these syntheses have as their condition a subject that is by rights distinct from the syntheses and of the contents that it produces[5]: the surface self as a psychological *analogon* of the Kantian transcendental I. The surface self must be able to accompany all our representations because it is the surface self that produces them.

The fundamental self, which is only encountered at a subrepresentational level, is entirely different. Unlike the surface self, it is not active. Certainly there are many acts or mental syntheses, but the fundamental self is not their agent; they are accomplished in but not by it. They are passive syntheses, or, if it is preferred, the syntheses of a passive self. Bergson sometimes expresses himself as if the self were active, but only to immediately withdraw all activity from it: "If [. . .] I

19

retain the recollection of the preceding oscillation together with the image of the present oscillation [. . .] I shall perceive one in the other, *each permeating the other and organising themselves* like the notes of a tune, so as to form what we shall call a continuous or qualitative multiplicity with no resemblance to number."[6] What characterizes the immediate givens is their organic development, their self-composition or self-organization at the heart of consciousness. The error would be to presuppose that every synthesis is the act of a subject or of an active Self.[7] It is not a self that constitutes qualitative multiplicities; on the contrary, it is they that *constitute the fundamental self*—insofar as it senses or is moved by what happens, by what acts on or in it. The self only gathers together the *effect* of these syntheses.[8] The self, continually individuated by effects that it fill it up and deepen it, is these very effects. This is the big difference between the surface self and the fundamental self: the first is the agent of quantitative multiplicities, whereas the second is the patient of qualitative multiplicities.

These two aspects of the self do not testify to a dissociation of personality but constitute the aborted doubling proper to the Bergsonian cogito. Oscillation here does not mean alternation or antagonism. One should not suppose that one shifts alternately from the passive to the active self, nor that they struggle with one another. On the contrary, passive and active are not mutually exclusive. Passivity is always contemporaneous with activity; it is its correlate. In Bergson, one is always active and passive at the same time. This is what Bergson says when he describes the two aspects of the self as being next to or on top of one another, or in any case parallel to and reciprocally ignorant of one another: "When we explicitly count units by stringing them along a spatial line, is it not the case that, *alongside* this addition of identical terms standing out from a homogeneous background, an organization of these units is going on in the depths of the soul."[9] Between the two aspects of the self is a relationship of coexistence. The fundamental self borders or accompanies the surface self like a phantom—unless, of course, it is the other way around, and the surface self is the "ghost" or the "colourless shadow projected"[10] by the fundamental self.

The initial problem is only reinforced: if the fundamental self is a passive self that only collects and conserves the qualitative variations that progressively individuate it, how can it become the free and active self that Bergson describes in the third chapter of *Time and Freewill*? By what miracle does the passive self of the depths become an active self—so active, even, that it takes over from the surface self and upsets its symbolic system of representations? If one supposes that it merely passively accompanies our activity in the depths of the soul, then how can it rise up to the surface? This problem cannot be resolved directly; it forces us to pass via a series of detours concerning first the method put to work by Bergson and then the status that he accords to number.

What has to be explained is the *fact* of freedom.[11] Such an undertaking might recall Kant, if in reality it didn't proceed by an entirely different method, close in many ways to Leibniz. From this point of view, one must recall the celebrated passage in *Matter and Memory* where Bergson gives an exposition of his method for the first time—and where he makes it clear that it was already at work in *Time and Freewill*:

> That which is commonly called a *fact* is not reality as it appears to immediate intuition, but an adaptation of the real to the interests of practice and to the exigencies of social life. Pure intuition, external or internal, is that of an undivided continuity. We break up this continuity into elements laid side by side, which correspond in the one case to distinct *words*, in the other to independent *objects*. [. . .] By unmaking that which these needs have made, we may restore to intuition its original purity and so recover contact with the real. [. . .] To give up certain habits of thinking, even of

perceiving, is far from easy: yet this is but the negative part of the work to be done; and when it is done, when we have placed ourselves at what we have called the *turn* of experience, when we have profited by the faint light which, illuminating the passage from the *immediate* to the *useful*, marks the dawn of our human experience, there still remains to be reconstituted, with the infinitely small elements which we thus perceive of the real curve, the curve itself stretching out into the darkness behind them. In this sense, the task of the philosopher, as we understand it, closely resembles that of the mathematician who determines a function by starting from the differential. The final effort of philosophical research is a true work of integration. We have already attempted to apply this method to the problem of consciousness.[12]

It is not a matter here of ascending from the fact to its conditions of possibility, in the Kantian manner. Rather, it is a matter, in conformity with its neo-Leibnizian inspiration, of determining the genetic elements that account for *such and such* a precise fact within immediate experience itself. It is the Bergsonian version of the principle of sufficient reason, according to which the concept must be no bigger than its object.[13] The problem is no longer one of establishing the conditions of possibility for all possible experience but rather of reconstituting the genetic source of each real experience, with the help of these "infinitely small elements" that Bergson talks of, veritable differentials of consciousness.[14] Such is how Bergson describes the immediate givens—or rather, that is how he would describe them if he were "some bold novelist, tearing aside the cleverly woven curtain of our conventional ego," thus indicating "under this juxtaposition of simple states an infinite permeation of a thousand different impressions which have already ceased to exist the instant they are named."[15] Each time the immediate givens are described as the grasping of a swarming of infinitesimal, vanishing elements that escape from the space of representation.

Everything happens as if in his own way Bergson replayed the classic opposition between Kant and Maïmon. The objections that Maïmon addresses to Kant are well known: he reproaches him with closing the system of representation on itself while positing a "thing itself" outside of it as an unknowable and unrepresentable object. Kant thus misunderstood the operations by which the understanding engenders sensible objects in a subterranean fashion. For Maïmon, this is because phenomena are the product of a summation of differentials that operates at a subrepresentational level. There is no longer any given—or rather the given gets infinitesimally small.[16] However, the differentials of phenomena are not given to intuition, as they have zero quantity ($dx = 0$, $dy = 0$). It is their relations (dy/dx) that engender the phenomena, which are given to intuition. "These differentials of objects are what one calls noumena, but the objects themselves that arise from them are phenomena. In relation to intuition, the differential of every object in itself = 0, $dx = 0$, $dy = 0$, etc. But their relations do not = 0, on the contrary, they can be indicated in a determinate manner in the intuitions that arise from them."[17] In the same gesture, the principle of continuity between the surface system of representation and the depths of the "thing in itself," which was missing in Kant, finds itself reestablished.

Maïmon is then led to dissociate two types of knowledge. On the one hand, is the common knowledge that submits a preexisting, preformed datum and object of intuition to the concepts of the understanding, establishing a discontinuity between intuition and concept. On the other is a knowledge that engenders the givens of experience according to particular rules (that is to say, according to their mode of differentials), thereby restoring the continuity that was lacking between intuition and concept.[18] In this case, "the understanding cannot think an object as if already formed but only in the process of its formation, that is to say, as a process."[19] Depending on the point of view, one discovers things in terms of the static aspect of a product already formed in intuition or in terms of the fluid or dynamic aspect of their production according to their mode of differential.[20] Is it not this same type of distinction that one rediscovers later in Bergson, when he criticizes the Kantian position and distinguishes two types of knowledge in terms that one could believe he had borrowed from Maïmon? "To say that knowledge comes from the subject and that this prevents the immediate givens from being objective is *a priori* to deny the possibility of two very different kinds of knowledge, one kind of knowledge that is static through concepts, the other dynamic, through immediate intuition, in which the act of knowing coincides with the act that generates reality."[21]

Does one not find these two modes of knowledge already at work in the distinction between the surface self and the fundamental self? The surface self is a self that can only think movement and speed as a function of "spaces once traversed and of simultaneous positions once reached." Everything that it thinks, it thinks in conformity with the principles of mechanics, insofar as "mechanics necessarily deals with equations, and that an algebraic equation always expresses something already done."[22] In other words, the surface self is not capable of engendering phenomena, although it can submit them to an indefinite number of rules of construction. The given is constructed or reconstructed, but not given, by the surface self. Only the other aspect of the self reaches these depths; it alone achieves properly genetic (and no longer nominal) definitions of phenomena, insofar as it merges with pure duration, the genetic source of all reality in Bergson. One gives a reason for a phenomenon insofar as one grasps it in its own duration because "it is of the very essence of duration and motion, as they appear to our consciousness, to be something that is unceasingly being done"[23] and to thereby make us glimpse the differential elements that one must then integrate as so many tendencies.

One will object that in the same passage Bergson criticizes the notion of the differential, which, however far it may go, never descends into the interval between two positions of a moving object—the very place in which movement happens—but is always situated at one of its extremities.[24] But one must distinguish between two conceptions, or rather two uses, of the differential in Bergson: a metaphysical and a scientific use. One must distinguish between the differential as noumenon or pure Idea of the understanding, such as it is glimpsed in the depths of experience, and the differential as a mathematical equation properly speaking. What is more, the repeated criticisms that Bergson addresses to the scientific uses of the differential seem destined to preserve the resources of a strictly metaphysical use of the differential, a use that makes "of philosophical research a veritable labor of integration." One sees it in *Matter and Memory*, when he conceives concrete perception as the "synthesis, made by memory, of an infinity of 'pure perceptions' which succeed each other,"[25] or in *Creative Evolution*, when he defines the élan vital as a current of consciousness charged with "an enormous multiplicity of virtualities"[26] that penetrate each other, or as an infinitesimal addition of little quantities of indetermination,[27] or even, in the *Two Sources*, when he describes the "whole of obligation" as the integral of the "thousand special habits that we have contracted of obeying the thousand special demands of social life."[28] In each case, the metaphysical use of the differential is distinguished from any scientific application.[29]

What difference is there from the one to the other? Doesn't the difference between them pass precisely via number? Isn't it the putting into the form of a differential equation, the transposition into space that number implies, the whole latent geometricism of mathematics, which constitutes the very limit of the scientific application? That is the sense of the conception of number that already appears in *Time and Freewill*. Such a conception doesn't only imply that number is conceived in an essential relationship with the extension that it measures, as in Descartes. It also implies that it can only be constructed on the condition that, as in Leibniz, the unities that it composes are situated in a space. In Leibniz, in effect, each unity is comparable to a situs in its relationship of coexistence with other situs: Leibnizian number isn't only the production of a synthesis but also of a specifically spatial synthesis as coexistence of ideally situated distinct unities. Bergson can then conclude from this, in a general manner, that "space is, accordingly, the material with which the mind builds up number and the medium in which the mind places it."[30]

Bergson's analysis supposes a restriction of analysis solely to the clear idea of number, to the precise extent that "every clear idea of number implies a visual image in space."[31] The clear idea of a number is the idea that it is "possible to divide the unit into as many parts as we like,"[32] that is to say, of seeing in the unity the possible divisions that one can carry out on it. There is only a clear vision because space renders these unities distinct or distinguishable from one another. But is that really the only idea of number in Bergson? Is there only one conception of number in *Time and Freewill*? Alongside this conception, does one not encounter an entirely different idea of number, no longer a clear idea but rather a confused, obscure one? Bergson can, in effect, say that qualitative multiplicities have "no affiliation with number," as they are pure heterogeneity.[33] He can even affirm, in categorical fashion, that "the multiplicity of conscious states, regarded in its original purity, is not at all like the discrete multiplicity which goes to form a number."[34]

However, several lines later, he adds that this multiplicity, this distinction, this heterogeneity, "contains the number potentially," in the sense that one is in the presence of multiplicities without any definite quantity. Consciousness operates a qualitative discrimination, yet it does so without counting the qualities or even making them *several*, Bergson clarifies.[35] When the fundamental self hears the striking of the clock, it doesn't count them, although it knows, confusedly, how many strikes have already sounded.[36] They are only several virtually because for the time being they only constitute one and the same qualitative process. If the fundamental self is incapable of counting, it is because it only has an obscure idea of number; it can only grasp number insofar as it participates in the quality. However, it remains possible to analyze its content and to enumerate the striking of the clock. It is in this sense that Bergson talks of "potential" number in the first place.[37]

But should we stop there? Are there not nondenumerable numbers, multiplicities that cannot be analyzed or for which the analysis is interminable and in vain? If the fundamental self is incapable of counting, must one not, inversely, say that the surface self is also incapable of counting the nondenumerable unities plunged in the depths because their analysis would be infinite, and so one can only speak in an approximate way of "thousands and thousands" of sensations, sentiments, or ideas?[38] For each of the two selves, for each of the two aspects of the personality, counting is impossible. Neither of the two selves can count the multiplicities of the other. If the fundamental self only has a *confused idea* of the number that a quantitative multiplicity forms, inversely, the surface self only has an *obscure idea* of the number that a qualitative multiplicity forms. Qualitative multiplicities are thus not deprived of any kinship with number. They testify to a different conception, a different idea of number: they are its obscure idea. Depth in Bergson means confused or obscure number.[39]

Had Leibniz not already indicated such a distinction? It is well known that Leibniz first defines number by its quality (its indivisible unity insofar as it is *such and such* number), rather than by its quantity or its magnitude. Certainly, as we have seen, each unity is comparable to a situs in its relationship of coexistence with other situs in an ideal space. But the point of view changes when Leibniz considers, for example, fractions or irrational numbers. Number is then defined less as a unity than as a relation. [40] The operation is no longer synthesis, as it is for whole numbers. Rather, it is an analysis that sometimes arrives at a last term and sometimes doesn't (taking into account the indeterminacy of its parts), as with the series decimal points for $\sqrt{2}$, for example.[41] In this latter case, it remains true that number can be expressed in extension (thus the diagonal of the square as the determinate representation of $\sqrt{2}$, or curves as the expression of a differential quotient[42]), but it can also be considered analogous to the spiritual unity of a monad, "the resolution of which goes on to infinity."[43] Number can thus sometimes be referred to discrete multiplicity *partes extra partes*, and sometimes to an unanalyzable intensive multiplicity, enveloped in the monad as a metaphysical point.[44] In Bergsonian terms, one must therefore say that there are two uses of the differential: a scientific or geometrical use (according to its clear idea) and a metaphysical use (according to its obscure idea).

◇◇◇◇◇◇◇◇◇◇◇◇◇◇◇◇◇◇◇◇◇

Hasn't this detour through method and number distanced us considerably from the problem of freedom? On the contrary, nothing brings us closer to it than the parallel with Leibniz, because the unanalyzable number enveloped in each monad is, for Leibniz, analogous to freedom. Leibniz often comes back to this point: it is with the help of mathematical considerations of the nature of the infinite that he affirms that he has resolved the problem of freedom.[45] Isn't this equally what happens in Bergson, albeit in an inverse form? One forgets too quickly that the question of freedom in *Time and Freewill* is posed on the basis of the examination of number, of two ideas of number—its clear idea (numerical multiplicity) and its obscure idea (qualitative multiplicity)—just as in Leibniz the examination of number constitutes the starting point for the question of freedom. The differential is the figure of freedom. The unforeseeability of the latter must first be sought in the infinitesimal quantities of indeterminacy of which qualitative multiplicities are the incessantly growing synthesis. Our freedom resides first of all in these thousands upon thousands of sentiments, thoughts, and perceptions of of which we *are* the synthesis. That is what must now be explained.

Certain commentaries have not failed to spot the resemblances between Leibniz's and Bergson's descriptions. In acting freely, the fundamental self rediscovers all the characteristics of a Leibnizian monad.[46] The free act is heavy with a whole past that expresses and represents the entire soul. "It is the whole soul, in fact, which gives rise to the free decision: and the act will be so much the freer the more the dynamic series with which it is connected tends to be the fundamental self."[47] The free act is the integral of the whole history of the person—the integral of its sentiments, its thoughts, and its aspirations.[48] There are numerous texts in which Leibniz, for his part, affirms that "in each substance there are traces of everything that has happened to it" and that "the perceptions which are found together in one soul at the same time include a veritably infinite multitude of little indistinguishable feelings, which the subsequent series must develop, so that we need not be astonished at the infinite variety of what must result from it in time."[49]

Bergson subsequently clarifies: appearing as irrational is proper to this dynamic series, taking into account a subterranean logic that expresses a sort of law of curvature: "We wish to know the reason why we have made up our mind, and we find that we have decided without any reason, and perhaps even against every reason. But, in certain cases, that is the best of reasons."[50] Even if the curve of this dynamic series necessarily has a reason for Leibniz, it can nevertheless appear as irrational as long as "there must be reasons, which are like abysses exceeding everything that creatures can grasp."[51] In one case as in the other, freedom is analogous to the obscure number of a curve that the whole person expresses by means of decisions and "free acts" that are sometimes incomprehensible. This curve is determined by a multiplicity of indistinguishable little sentiments, to speak like Leibniz, by "emotions [that] are instinct with a thousand sensations, feelings or ideas which pervade them," to speak like Bergson.[52]

Does one not rediscover here the differential element that we have been seeking since the beginning? Is that not what we rediscover at the heart of the immediate givens? Is it not in fact emotion that constitutes the differential element of freedom in Bergson, even if one must not conclude too quickly from the one to the other? To understand this link, what emotion consists of must be defined more precisely. Two misunderstandings are to be avoided. The first would be to believe that emotion is one affection among others. Emotion is not one particular type of qualitative multiplicity; every qualitative multiplicity is emotion. Better still, it is emotion that ensures the qualitative character of experience. One should say, like Dewey, that "experience is emotional, but there are not separate things in it called emotions."[53] That is why Bergson can speak of emotion even in the case of scarcely moving experiences such as hearing a clock strike the hour.[54] In Bergson, emotion is coloring or musical insofar as it qualifies the whole of an experience; suddenly a new nuance of sadness or joy constitutes the integral of the moment. Emotion ensures that each experience has its own proper tonality, its nuance. In this sense, it is always immediately aesthetic.[55]

At the level of immediate givens, we are all novelists, musicians, or painters. It is well known—and creators know this better than anyone—that to express what is properly qualitative about a whole, one would have to include everything that makes it up. One would have to describe everything that belongs to such and such a precise moment—not just the forms of the landscape, but what it is populated with, such as changing sounds, noises, talking, light, heat, profound states of the soul, infinitesimal variations of sentiment, and so on—in short, the obscure number of the quality. This is another way of saying that one is only ever moved by a whole, that the whole is this emotion itself. That is the second misunderstanding to avoid: we are supposedly moved because there is, within whatever multiplicity, an object that particularly touches us. But nothing is less true: we are never moved first of all by an object but instead by the whole within which this object then appears as a crystallization. At least this is the case for every deep emotion. That is the reason why, from the beginning of *Time and Freewill*, Bergson takes care to distinguish genuine emotion, profound emotion, from all the surface emotions, those that are determined precisely by external objects and that only provoke a surface agitation.[56] The second misunderstanding, then, would be to suppose what is perceived provokes emotions in us and to introduce a causal relation here. The whole of *Time and Freewill* is an essay against causality, in favor of another kind of relation, of the suggestion, influence, or "psychic attraction"[57] type. The relation is not one of causation but of expression: emotion expresses the qualitative unity proper to each experience, and this is how it is qualitatively distinguished from the others.

A text that almost makes Bergson the "bold novelist" that he calls for with all his might, even as it testifies to a barely hidden use of the infinitesimal, must be cited here in its entirety:

> An involuntary allusion, a word of blame from an authorized mouth, can throw us into the sadness in which, unhappy with ourselves and despairing of the future, we believe that we see all the avenues of life closing down before us. And just as the infinitesimally small crystal falling into the supersaturated solution calls unto itself the immense multitude of scattered molecules, immediately transforming the transparent liquid into an opaque and solid mass, so, with the faintest sound of a reproach falling amongst them, all the apparently vanquished timidities, momentarily consoled disillusionment, floating sadnesses, which were only awaiting an opportunity so as to crystallize

into a compact mass, come running from here, there and everywhere, from a thousand different points and go by all the paths to the heart, weighing down heavily on a soul which is now inert and discouraged. This somewhat sickly sensibility is a rare thing, happily; but who hasn't felt their amour propre painfully touched, on certain occasions, and the lease of life they could have taken arrested, instead of being penetrated by a delightful harmony, because a word whispered into the ear, insinuating its way into the soul, reaching down into its most secret of recesses, has come to touch this hidden fiber which cannot resonate without all the powers of being trembling with it and vibrating in unison?[58]

It is the sum of all these emotions that constitutes the depth of the self—or rather that constitutes the self as a single deep emotion or "fundamental emotion." The fundamental self is the synthesis of all the emotions that compose it, the memory of all the "secret recesses" of its personality. But what is emotion itself the synthesis of? Bergson's text illustrates it here in an exemplary manner: emotion is the synthesis of the movements it vibrates to internally. It is not movement itself—or if it is, it is only insofar as it accompanies or prolongs the movement of what is happening elsewhere. It is a virtual movement that doubles the real movement of the world. If Bergson later defines virtual movement as a "demand for creation,"[59] it is because it is a demand for expression. It is all these infinitesimal, nearly insignificant demands, grasped in themselves, that will constitute the spiritual energy of which the free act will then be the expression. Obscurely, the fundamental self senses these virtual movements accumulate and this demand grow inside it. It is not without analogy to the plant of *Creative Evolution*, which, through its passive syntheses, accumulates an energy that comes from mineral elements drawn from the atmosphere, from the earth and from water, but that it never converts into movement for itself. For the plant, movement remains virtual and is only actualized in the animal: "Made of very complex molecules holding a considerable amount of chemical energy in the potential states [plants] are like explosives which only need a spark to set free the energy stored within them."[60] Is this not the very definition of emotions such as they accumulate in the depths of the self? And isn't the fundamental self what fills up with a spiritual energy that the surface self will be called on to make explode in a free creation? In this sense, the free act is activated by all the accumulated passivity.

For its part, the surface self does not allow itself to be moved by these confused wholes. It decomposes them into distinct parts according to the demands of all the different social, material, and intellectual orders. It does not allow itself to be moved by the ringing of the alarm clock; it only draws from it the imperative to get up and start a day of obligations. In this sense, the surface self only ever has partial perceptions, which it links to one another so as to compose wholes of another nature. If the fundamental self is the self of confused wholes and of merged parts, then the surface self is the self of distinct parts and composed wholes. In Bergson, profound/deep means total, while surface means partial. With the surface self, we are no longer on the side of the Aesthetic but of the Analytic: from the whole, we cut out "objects" that act on us and on which we act; symmetrically, this interaction makes "subjects" of us.

Whereas our self is interested in the parts that it composes and decomposes according to the imperatives of social life, these wholes continue to move it and accumulate in the depths. Doubtless these emotions would incite us to act, or rather to express the sadness of joy that they envelop, but they are prevented from doing so precisely by the demands of social life, which oblige us to interest ourselves in external objects and the causal relations that link us to these objects. We are constantly sacrificing the emotion of the wholes to the attention to parts. This is because the social world demands of us a certain type of perception, a certain type of action, of reaction, opinion, and even emotion, the partial character of which supposes the repression of deep emotions, those to which we vibrate at a subterranean level. We become "conscious automata" because we have "everything to gain in being so,"[61] with the body subjected to the regularity of habits (sensorimotor montages) and thinking subjected to mechanical chains of association (an associationist mechanics for the uniformity of associative chains).

Social life in effect presupposes innumerable infinitesimal coercions, repressions, and repudiations of sensibility, its expressive potential (the aesthetic plane) crushed and occulted thousands upon thousands of times, but it also presupposes infinitesimal shames, compromises, or cowardlinesses that offend our "particular conception of life"[62] (the ethical plane). One cannot understand Bergson's conception of freedom without first measuring to what point the system of social life in us is opposed to every form of (ethical or aesthetic) expression. One is only prevented from acting freely to the extent that one is first prevented from expressing freely. That is why freedom in Bergson is not so much a freedom of action as a freedom of expression and creation. Certainly Bergson does not stop talking about the "free act," but to act is not to commit to an action; initially it is to express or create. At first the man who acts freely is the one who expresses what until then could not be expressed, taking into account the demands of all sorts that weighed on him. Freedom is a creation of the self by the self, and the free man is analogous to an artist or a superior moralist. "We are free when our acts spring from our whole personality, when they express it, when they have that indefinable resemblance to it which one sometimes finds between the artist and his work."[63]

It is necessary to recall this immense crushing, without which the genesis of freedom in Bergson remains incomprehensible and arises as if by a miracle. If not, one will not understand in what way freedom constitutes a revolt, an uprising of the infinitesimal that at last comes to answer for us. One understands even less from where the fundamental self draws its volcanic strength, which allows it to loosen or break the system of social obligations without this accumulation of unexpressed emotions, which together vindicate a right to expression. Everything happens as if the world let us occupy no other position or rhythm of duration than those that its present imposes on us. There is more anger than one imagines in Bergson—not so much against social life itself as against ourselves, against our own "sluggishness or indolence," against this "strange reluctance to exercise our will" that makes us abdicate our freedom: "It will be found that the majority of our daily actions are performed in this way and that, owing to the solidification in memory of such and such sensations, feelings or ideas, impressions from the outside call forth movements on our part which, though conscious and even intelligent, have many points of resemblance with reflex acts. [. . .] Moreover we will grant to determinism that we often resign our freedom in more serious circumstances, and that, by sluggishness or indolence, we allow this same local process to run its course when our whole personality ought, so to speak, to vibrate."[64]

One must accept the consequences of the preceding from the point of view of Bergson's conception of memory. One sees that for most of the time emotions lead a life of expectation. Emotion is not just memory, or rather memory is not just memory in Bergson. On another plane, it is expectation—pure expectation. Our conscious life leans on an unconscious expectation, which is like a memory of the spirit/mind,[65] a memory-spirit. It isn't a matter of the memory of what we have lived through and of which a recollection has been conserved; rather, it is a matter of the memory of what we have been prevented from living, whatever the reason may be. We can live our ordinary life, be as busy as ever, but it nonetheless remains that the fundamental self is waiting and does nothing but wait, until the moment when all this accumulated expectation is crystallized on an object or a propitious situation, through which it expresses itself.[66] The self hadn't stopped being virtually present, analogous at every point with a name that one doesn't manage to retrieve and obeying the same paradoxical functioning. There is, in effect, a paradox of the forgotten name: *we know perfectly well which name it is a matter of* because we know that none of those that have come to mind are appropriate, but in parallel, *we are totally unaware of which name it is a matter* because that is precisely what we are looking for—except that here it is not a matter of a name but of ourselves. The fundamental self pushes at the edges of the surface self with the same insistence and indetermination as the name that we have on the tip of our tongue, known perfectly by and completely unknown to us at one and the same time, at once both properly singular (because it is what is most personal to us) and completely indeterminate.[67] We are haunted by ourselves. The fundamental self is the phantom of freedom.

One rediscovers here the mutual ignorance of the two aspects of the self, the difference of nature that separates them, each one developing, so to speak, against the other. Bergson will not stop rediscovering and deepening this scission, for which he will formulate the law of development in the *Two Sources*: "Experience shows that if, in the case of two contrary but complementary tendencies, we find one to have grown until it tries to monopolize all the room, the other will profit by this, provided it has been able to survive; its turn will come again, and it will then benefit by everything which has been done without its aid, which has even been energetically developed in specific *opposition* to it."[68] That is how the two aspects of the self are: side by side and one against the other. If the surface self wins the first time around, pushing the other self into the depths of forgetting, "it is not rare that a revolt is produced" and for the fundamental self to shoot back up again with a strength that is all the greater for having suffered containment for too long. In this sense, freedom in Bergson is always a liberation.

The fundamental self has to rise back up to the surface so as to remind us of its existence, as if the differ-ence between the two selves testified to a difference of nature at the heart of memory. Everything in effect hap-pens as if there were two memories: on the one hand, the *intellectual* and habitual memory that Bergson ex-plores in *Matter and Memory*; on the other, the *spiritual* memory that he rediscovers with *Creative Evolution*. On the one hand, a memory that is inactive by nature, al-ways partial, which only becomes active so as to re-spond to the incessant demands of the present;[69] on the other, a total, intensive memory that is always silently active, the integral of which is the élan for life itself and which answers to the future. On the one hand, a mem-ory of what we have known or lived through and which gives to each present its signification; on the other, a memory of what we are and which gives to time its ori-entation. Once again, without the latter, without the energy that it continually fills up with, the sense of the future remains incomprehensible in Bergsonism. It is what constitutes the sense of the future in us.

In Bergson, intuition relies on this spiritual, essen-tially virtual, memory. It is from these depths that intu-ition draws its "spiritual energy." That is the conclusion that the *Two Sources* will reach. Intuition originates in a fundamental emotion, generative of ideas. "There are emotions which beget thought; and invention, though it belongs to the category of the intellect, may partake of sensibility in its substance. [. . .] An emotion is an affective stirring of the soul, but a surface agitation is one thing, an upheaval of the depths another."[70] One emotion, and one alone, is enough for it to form a mass out of all the others that feed it and to grow enough to form a tendency or a demand for creation that is suf-ficiently strong to overthrow the system of the surface self. "The soul within which this demand dwells may indeed have felt it fully only once in a lifetime, but it is always there, a unique emotion, an impulse, an élan received from the very heart of things."[71] The three el-ements of Bergsonism are recovered: *duration*, which animates the depth of things; profound *emotion* conserved in a memory of the future; and the *spirit*, which receives all its energy, permitting it to open time up to a creative duration.

So the only freedom is of the spirit. Only spirit needs to be liberated in Bergson, and what it has to be liberated from is the intelligence. If the intelligence can in turn be free, it will only be so by the spirit, which its effort at intuition feeds. That is how one can open up to levels of reality that exceed the intelligence properly so called. But can one really speak of opening? Isn't intuition what remains closed in on itself? Doesn't Bergson in effect define intuition as an exclusive relation of the spirit with itself? Is it not above all a reflection of the spirit on itself, turning toward what is most vanishing in it? What would be threatened, then, is not freedom but the method of intuition—unless intuition was itself accompanied by a properly spiritual affect, one capable of opening up to other realities, other rhythms of duration.

Intuition and Sympathy

Bergson the Perspectivist

> The philosopher neither obeys nor commands,
> he seeks to sympathise.
> —*Bergson*

What does Bergson's "sympathy" mean in relation to the subject of intuition? It belongs to that set of general and undefined terms that, rather than illuminate, seem to obscure the Bergsonian method. Commentators rarely evoke it, other than to diminish its importance. The term "sympathy" would thus only be used so as to illustrate the intuitive act or "series of acts" that would themselves found a rigorous method. One rapidly comes to the conclusion that intuition can only be rigorously conceptualized as a method if it ceases to be conceived as sympathy, a vague notion too heavily marked by psychology. Sympathy would basically be nothing but a concession made to pedagogy or psychology, a substitute intuition.

Yet we know that Bergson constantly returns to the point that intuition and sympathy seem to be confused: "We call intuition here the *sympathy* by which one is transported into the interior of an object in order to coincide with what there is unique and consequently inexpressive in it."[1] Similarly, aesthetic intuition is replaced "within the object by a kind of sympathy."[2] Elsewhere intuition is defined as a "spiritual sympathy" with what

39

is "innermost" in a reality.[3] Sympathy here seems to be more than an illustration of intuition or a vague psychological correlate. It appears instead as an indispensable methodological complement. It is sympathy that allows one to pass into the "interior" of realities, to grasp them from "inside," to get into the very point of view of such and such reality. It testifies to a profound perspectivism that is proper to Bergson. But what does it mean to "pass into," to "grasp from the inside"? Does this give a gain in precision and rigor? More importantly, if Bergson identifies sympathy and intuition with one another, why return specifically to sympathy? How is it distinct from "acts" of intuition properly so called? Does it have a distinct methodological status? Such a question is decisive for the place and function of affect in a strictly philosophical method.

Bergson initially gives rather vague indications: intuition is a long labor that calls for assiduous acquaintance with the object: "For one does not obtain from reality an intuition, that is to say, a spiritual harmony with its innermost quality, if one has not gained its confidence by a long comradeship with its superficial manifestations."[4] Certainly we can suppose that for the moment it is only a matter of preparatory conditions, which are still empirical. But the essential point is already played out at this level. Reality is constituted as a continuous whole that quickly possesses an internal unity (the "fusion" of the "mass" [of ideas]). Now the whole owes its nature as a whole to a certain memory, which ensures the internal continuity of which it is made up. In other words, this long acquaintance allows the leap that is proper to the intuitive act, which Bergson makes clear is neither synthesis nor recollection, to be accomplished. What does this leap consist of? It is that the spirit, by an effort on itself, doesn't only install itself "immediately" in the element of duration but in that of sense too.[5] The duration of this reality is not without memory nor without a kind of consciousness, characterized as an intention or direction constitutive of sense. Thus, at the end of this preparatory labor, the reality under consideration becomes real duration at the same time as it expresses an intention, a direction that constitutes it as a virtual consciousness. What is specifically due to the labor of intuition is the grasping of this reality as duration, but what is properly due to sympathy is the grasping of an intention internal to this duration. It is even possible that the conception of duration as memory can only be understood by the intermediary of this act of sympathy. That is what must now be explained.

Intuition bears exclusively on totalities that are so many substantivized adjectives: the vital, the material, the social, the personal, and so on. This amounts to saying that it circulates through the entire universe (monism), the different levels of which it traverses (pluralism). However, Bergson affirms that intuition is the "direct vision of the mind by the mind."[6] He insists on this point: intuition is never anything other than a "reflection" of the mind on itself.[7] Intuition in Bergson is not sensible intuition, with which in any case it has complex links.[8] Thus there is no intuition of matter, of life of society as such, that is to say, as substantives. How, then, can intuition open up to other levels of reality and attain such extension? It proceeds by sympathy. In a manner that is still abstract, one can define sympathy as the movement by means of which each one of these realities becomes "mind." How is such a transformation possible? One can easily conceive how a mind can enter "into sympathy" with itself or with another mind. Bergson frequently invokes a sort of psychological endosmosis, a reciprocal penetration of minds. He gives an example in *The Creative Mind* when he attempts to set out an equivalent of Berkeley's fundamental intuition, beyond the theses effectively deposited in language. He goes back to a primordial intention of which his oeuvre would be the indirect expression.[9] At this level, sympathy is defined as the movement by which one endeavors to rejoin a purely spiritual intention, immanent to the whole (here Berkeley's oeuvre) and of which it will be as if the integral.

This movement is verified when one changes level. Is it not the same movement that is in effect produced when one descends to the vital level? One endeavors to grasp the primordial intention of life, beyond the variety of living forms; this is the very sense of the concept of élan. Élan is not only destined to describe life as the "unforeseeable upsurge of novelty," but it is also what allows the continuous whole of the vital to be grasped as mind or consciousness in the first place. In other words, the vital ceases to be external to the sphere of the spirit, which is what explains that intuition can henceforth take it as an object, in conformity with its definition, as it is a matter of a profound relation of the spirit with one of its deepest levels. Or rather, thanks to sympathy, life becomes a "subject" for metaphysics (as spirit or consciousness), whereas it remains an "object" for science (as physicochemical material). Sympathy plays an essential role here: it frees up the properly spiritual "intention" of the vital, thus allowing it to be consisted as a subject tendency within metaphysics. In the same move, it seems to render it accessible to intuition.

But if one can lend life an intention, free up the spiritual élan that animates it, then can one proceed in the same way with matter? How is the spiritual element of matter, which by definition is lacking any spirituality, to be extracted? Here too the concept of intuition would not by itself allow this extension to be understood if it didn't establish a sympathy with matter. What does it consist of at this level? It is defined by establishing a community of movements. The spiritual element of matter is movement as indivisible reality. The spirit "sympathizes" with matter insofar as it grasps it, not as thing or mass but as pure movement; consequently, the continuous whole of matter becomes spirit or consciousness as "pure perception." This is the central operation of the first and fourth chapters of *Matter and Memory*:

a matter reduced to movement but thereby promoted to the status of virtual consciousness.[10] In this sense, one can say that élan is to the vital image what image or pure perception is to the material universe: the mark of a sympathy.

However, the response is still incomplete, because what is properly spiritual in movement? Is it the image? Pure perception? That wouldn't explain anything because these terms suppose what is in question. Certainly the image is defined as the pure or actual perception of movement, but how is such a definition possible? Intuition must here be reintroduced in its "fundamental" sense: "thinking intuitively is thinking in duration."[11] What constitutes the spirit of matter is its duration. "We place consciousness at the heart of things for the very reason that we credit them with a time that endures."[12] Duration is the spiritual element of the material (and all the more so of the vital or the social). That is why science can attain movement, but without being able to extract the mobility that is its essence: it doesn't think (in terms of) duration. Duration primarily signifies conservation. Duration exists once an instant, however brief it may be, conserves what it receives from the previous instant, even if only to transmit it immediately—so much so that what might by rights be like a memory (conservation) should instead be thought as a forgetting that allows material movement to go on indefinitely without loss (communication): "We can bestow upon this memory just what is needed to make the connection; it will be, if we like, this very connection, a mere continuing of the before into the immediate after with a perpetually renewed forgetfulness of what is not the immediately prior moment."[13] What matters here is that one cannot think matter without making a kind of memory (forgetting) or (unconscious) consciousness intervene. This is the ultimate limit of sympathy, the point where the spirit becomes an immense unconscious forgetting. Matter is a consciousness that is blocked, a memory that is aborted. Intuition, thought in duration, would not have been able to establish itself without sympathy, the function of which is to allow him or it to posit the fundamental Bergsonian identity: duration = memory = mind.[14]

We wanted to distinguish sympathy as such, but here we find ourselves led back to intuition as its foundation. What is more, if duration is immediately memory, if memory is immediately consciousness, and if terms end up being identified with one another, why maintain a special status for sympathy? Cannot intuition conclude by itself from duration to consciousness? Does it not grasp one and the same continuous reality, which it will call, indifferently, duration, memory, or consciousness, depending on the context? In this case there is no need to have recourse to sympathy. But that is only true when the spirit has a "direct vision" of itself, in conformity with the definitions of intuition given earlier. Once it apprehends other realities, the relation necessarily becomes indirect. It is here that it needs to be prolonged into sympathy, because sympathy is something different from a fusion without distance, which would assimilate it roughly to an intuitive act. Rather, it rests on reasoning by analogy.[15] That is one of its essential differences from intuition. It possesses the same rigor as classical analogy, although it founds its reasoning on the same principles.

It is well known that classical analogy is defined as a proportion, that is to say, as an equality of relations $(A/B = C/D)$, the function of which consists in establishing a resemblance among differing terms. It is already encountered in Plato, in whom the analogical structure of proportion remains static. "We contrive to find resemblances between things in spite of their diversity, and to take a stable view of them in spite of their instability. [. . .] All this is the work of man."[16] It only becomes dynamic with the introduction of an Idea toward which terms are spiritually orientated, in proportion to their resemblance with it "running, as it were, after themselves, to coincide with the immutability of the Idea."[17] In other words, the introduction of an Idea converts the static structure into a dynamic series, if only to then lose its initial analogical character.[18] One thereby passes from the science of measure to the science of harmony, transforming analogy into a sort of sympathy or friendship, a *philia*.[19] In Plato, the passage from static analogy to dynamic series marks the passage from geometrical science to philosophy properly so called, as a dialectic of Ideas.

How is Bergsonian analogy distinguished from classical analogy? It is its rigorous inverse because it isn't founded on terms but on movements. In Bergson, analogy only exists among movements. It is thus no longer structured by a measure, because "movement is not measurable, and the function of science is to measure."[20] One thus no longer raises oneself up from science to philosophy. Rather, only the metaphysician, from the start and without the help of any science, can have recourse to analogical reasoning because he alone can attain movements as such. Perhaps at its beginning differential calculus attempted to measure these dynamisms, but we have seen that because of the remnants of geometry it contained, it was condemned to thinking in symbolic terms.[21] If Bergsonian analogy is an analogy among tendencies, then that means it does not structure the similar but instead the common.[22] It is no longer a matter of an external *resemblance* among relations but of an internal *communication* among tendencies or movements.[23]

How is such a reversal possible? It is because the Idea is now no longer external to the terms that it arranges. Not only has it passed into them, but it also constitutes their interiority in the form of an "intention." Each tendency is the actualization of its Idea, which is also the "pure memory" from which it originates.[24] In this sense, the tendency is subject, insofar as it possesses its principle of development in itself, instead of being separated from it. In any case, that is why the development of tendency in Bergson consists ultimately in going back to the "original source" from which it comes.

It goes back to its principle as if toward what is most internal and spiritual to it, toward the fundamental emotion from which it originates.[25] One goes back into the past but one is never shrinking back; on the contrary, it allows a greater opening up of the future. That is the fundamental proportion in Bergson: the opening up of the future is proportional to the quantity of the past that comes to be inserted into the present action. As Deleuze says, there is Platonic tone in Bergson: the Idea as reminiscence or pure recollection.[26]

But if sympathy rests on indirect reasoning, how can it be associated with intuition? Can intuition be anything other than the "direct vision" that defines it? How can Bergson think of them as quasi-synonymous? We must make clear here the nature of the analogical reasoning to which he ceaselessly has recourse. Analogy is only made between our own internal movements and the movements of the universe in general. We first discover that we are spiritual, vital, material, intuitively, by plunging deep into ourselves: "The matter and life which fill the world are equally within us; the forces which work in all things we feel within ourselves; whatever may be the inner essence of what is and what is done, we are of that essence. Let us then go down into our own inner selves: the deeper the point we touch, the strong will be the thrust which sends us back up to the surface. Philosophical intuition is this contact, philosophy is this impetus [élan]."[27] One recognizes here the movement of intuition but also the foundation of analogy. Analogies are always established dynamically among our own tendencies, intuitively perceived, and those of the (social, vital, material, etc.) universe, concluded projectively. We are analogous to the universe (intuition); inversely, the universe is analogous to us (sympathy).[28] Analogy covers the vast domain in Bergson of the *as if.*

Bergson refrains from anthropomorphism. Sympathy is not an auxiliary to the storytelling function. The universe is not endowed with even a modified human movement, memory, or consciousness. On the contrary, it is man who, thanks to intuition, enters into "contact" with the nonhuman movements, memories, and consciousness deep inside him. There is basically [*au fond*] nothing human about man.[29] It is because intuition reaches the nonhuman tendencies in man that it can give the reciprocal impression of humanizing the nonhuman. But let us repeat the point: it was first necessary that [intuition] sought deep inside man the nonhuman tendencies that constitute him. In any case, that is why intuition calls for so long and difficult a labor: it is necessary to be transported to the sometimes inferior, sometimes superior limits of human experience to reach the pure material, vital, social, personal, and spiritual places across which man is composed.[30] Such a method effectively demands "that our faculties of observation tend towards the point, sometimes, of going beyond themselves (so as to arrive at a grasp, on the edge of the unconscious, of this 'pure perception' and this 'pure memory,' which are far from being [. . .] simple constructions of the mind)."[31] Our human condition—with its good sense and intelligence, with all the mixtures that it constructs so as to act on matter—prevents us from perceiving them integrally. That is why the integral can only be constructed artificially. One must in effect "reconstitute, with the infinitely small elements which we thus perceive of the real curve, the curve itself stretching out into the darkness behind them."[32]

The error of Kantianism is not to have perceived that the conditions of possibility that it posited were themselves conditioned by more obscure, more distant "sources," only accessible to an intuition that called for a turning away from science and the operative conditions to which Kant remained attached. Before knowing, the subject is matter, life, society, mind, person. What is more, it only knows because it is all these things at once. These totalities constitute the essential discovery of intuition, provided that it descends "more or less to the bottom of a same ocean,"[33] to the point that man is required to humanize and personalize the nonhuman totalities that traverse him at different levels of tension. The anthropological level is caught between continuous realities that are much more vast than it is, at inferior or superior levels, that tighten up and condense when they enter into the human form properly so called.[34] The human in Bergson is humanization—or rather humanization itself oscillates perpetually between dehumanization and overhumanization [*surhumanization*], depending on the different levels at which one grasps it and the different tendencies that act in it.

Does this allow us to better understand why Bergson calls analogical reasoning "sympathy"? We said that the function of classical analogy was to introduce resemblances within what differs, thus according an evident primacy to the sensible. Bergsonian analogy apparently proceeds no differently. It consists in finding what there is of the "spirit" or of "consciousness" within a given reality, thereby determining what it has in common with *us*. But that is only possible because intuition has previously determined what we have in common with *it*. Primacy is in reality accorded to alterity, to the dissimilar: it is because the other—the nonhuman—is in us that one can encounter it externally in the form of consciousness or intention. We project our own alterity. If it doesn't seem foreign to us (although each time it is a matter of an original discovery, and for this reason of a reality that we were unaware of having within us before acceding to it intuitively), it is thanks to the sympathy that we have established with ourselves and that has familiarized us with these alterities deep inside us in such a way that analogy seems to go from an other (in us) to an other (external to us) so as to situate them on a common plane. Strictly speaking, it is no longer a "human fabrication." That is why it is definitively a matter of an internal community and no longer of an external resemblance.

The importance of analogy in Bergson allows us to explain the criticism that he makes of it starting with *Time and Freewill*. If analogical reasoning or projection is founded when it proceeds on the basis of intuition, then it becomes an object of criticism when it proceeds on the basis of habit or reasoning: "We here put our finger on the mistake of those who regard pure duration as something that is similar to space but of a more simple nature."[35] How can one not see here once again a critique of the Kantian position? Yet everything starts well in Kant's exposition of the transcendental aesthetic, from a Bergsonian point of view. Inner sense is defined as the "the intuition of ourselves and of our inner states." Kant even makes it clear that to the extent that this "inner intuition yields no shape, we endeavor to make for this want by analogies. We represent the time-sequence by a line progressing to infinity."[36] At this stage Kant does not fail to recognize the irreducibility of time to space. But when the exposition of the three syntheses of inner sense intervenes, Kant reintroduces time as a line, reinforcing this concept as one passes from one synthesis to the next—so much so that succession is finally only conceived as addition or numbering. In other words, time can only become the object of knowledge by representation or figuring in external sense.[37] That is what *Time and Freewill* targets, via the distinction of the two types of multiplicity: the spatial and the temporal. Yet the danger doesn't come so much from the habit that we have of projecting "time into space"[38] as of the inverse introjection: "As the repeated picture of one identical objective phenomenon, ever recurring, cuts up our superficial psychic life into parts external to one another, the moments which are thus determined determine in their turn distinct segments in the dynamic and undivided progress of our more personal conscious states. Thus the mutual exteriority of which material objects gain from their juxtaposition in homogeneous space reverberates and spreads into the depths of consciousness."[39] It is because analogy is no longer based on an internal community of movements but rather on a reciprocal externalization of terms. Kantian analogy—or its equivalents—is in the first place not projective but introjective.[40]

In any case, we must clarify what Bergson understands by the terms "exterior" and "interior." One recalls that sympathy is not only sympathy for others but already for oneself, so much is it true that we too must pass into our interior.[41] "We are internal to ourselves and our personality is what we should know best. Yet such is not the case; our mind is as if it were in a strange home, whereas matter is familiar to it and in it the mind is at home."[42] One can see that the notions of "interior" and "exterior" do not testify to any ontological difference. There is no preexisting external world any more than there is a constituent internal world. Rigorously speaking, one ought not to speak of an internal world, as one can remain external to oneself. Similarly, one ought not to speak of an external world but of a tendency that produces the world as external. The exteriority to itself of perception poses the world as external and renders us external to ourselves. Inversely, it is a perception internal to itself that allows the passage to the inside of the world called "external." It tends to be identified with duration insofar as this latter is conserved in itself. The expression "in itself" has rarely had as many meanings as it does in Bergson, as it allows things to have a veritable interiority attributed to them. The "in itself" no longer designates that by which things will never be for us, but that by which they are also in us. It is in us that they remain in themselves because it is necessary to quit the framework of subjectivity.[43] It is well known that internal and external ought not to designate preexisting worlds but divergent tendencies— tension and extension—that are exercised in the two worlds. Ontology shifts from constituted worlds to their constitutive sources.

If there is one book that takes up and illustrates the entirety of the process that we have just described, it is *Creative Evolution*, which Bergson presents as an attempt at applying his method.[44] What is the starting point of the book? Bergson begins by describing creative evolution such as it is produced in us at each moment of duration. It is a matter of considering oneself intuitively in duration as a continuous whole. The whole question is, then, to know if one can pass from the observation of this creative evolution within us to a creative evolution without us. Can the spirit come out of this reflection on itself? This question leads Bergson to distinguish two types of totalities, systems closed artificially by the intelligence and naturally open wholes, in such a way as to then be able to give a rigorous foundation to analogical reasoning.[45] From the point of view of intuition, comparison can effectively only be made among open totalities, as they are the ones that endure.

All the criticisms that he then addresses to evolutionism in his conception of evolution follow on from this, as do all those that he addresses to mechanism and to finalism in their conception of creation. Evolutionism has not succeeded in thinking evolution, and mechanism and finalism have not succeeded in thinking what was creative about it, because their analogical reasoning was ill-founded every time: they reduce all the open wholes of nature onto the closed systems of the intelligence. Bergson proposes the exactly inverse operation. As Deleuze says, classical analogy changes its meaning; it is no longer "the whole that closes like an organism, it is the organism that opens onto a whole, like this virtual whole."[46] Bergson even goes further: he makes the tools of his method descend into life itself. Despite the divergence of the tendencies that divide it, does not life define itself as a whole that is at the same time sympathetic and analogous to itself? It is sympathetic to itself because different species can penetrate one another on the inside, like the insect that knows—as if it had always known—where to sting its prey in order to paralyze it, thereby testifying to the presence of a sort of common memory.[47] It is analogous to itself because on lines of evolution that have nothing to do with one another, one nevertheless discovers similar "intentions" (thus the formation of the eye).

One can then understand that the method utilized by Bergson wants to proceed like life itself. The philosopher is like the insect, which sympathetically divines its prey, with this difference: it doesn't deal with predators or prey but with essences or tendencies, with what is properly vital within the living thing. His knowledge is no longer the same as in the animal. It has become intuition—that is to say, a dilated instinct, which is no longer limited to the internal knowledge of a special object.[48] Intuition thus reveals us as participating in the great current of life, and it makes us experience what is vital in us.[49] Symmetrically, it discovers that life participates in consciousness. Led by this intuition, the study of the living—at the intersection of embryology, naturalism, paleontology, and so on—teaches us what is strictly vital in us, beyond the representation that the intelligence gives us of life and of ourselves. It makes us communicate with something that goes beyond it: the emotion of experiencing oneself as living.

One will perhaps perceive more precisely what the fundamental movement of sympathy, but also intuition, consists of. Both can now perhaps receive a distinct definition: intuition is that which enters into contact with the other in us (the material, the vital, the social); in this sense, it remains a relationship of self to self and cannot be anything else. Inversely, sympathy enters into relation with another. One can even say that it enters into this other by projecting our interiority into it; it detects a direction, an intention, a consciousness in it. These are equally the movements of our own inner alterity. If the spirit can become matter—by intuition— then matter can become spirit—by sympathy. If the spirit can become life, then life can become mind. If social can become mind, then mind can become social. If mind can become person, then person can become mind. One thereby retains the definition of intuition as the "direct vision of mind by mind," except that what the mind sees within itself are the diverse durations of matter, life, society, and so on. Symmetrically, sympathy "sees" in matter, life, and society a "consciousness" and an "intention" that is the manifestation of the plasticity of the mind according to its different levels of tension. However, is not this double movement the sign that one finds oneself enclosed within a sort of circle, a hypothesis reinforced by the perfect symmetry whereby they relaunch one another? Doesn't the possibility of making them almost synonymous come, finally, from the fact that they reciprocally presuppose one another?

We can only respond to this objection via a brief detour. We said that Bergson poses the identity as duration = memory = mind. But until now we have scarcely evoked the specific role of memory in this process. How is one not to see in this double movement the illustration of one of Bergson's most profound analyses, that concerning attentive recognition? How is one not to see the establishment not of a circle but of a circuit in analogical reasoning, a circuit comparable to that of the work of the intelligence described in *Matter and Memory* and then in *Mind-Energy*? One can even say that the leap of intuition and the élan of sympathy break open as many circles as they affirm the depth of their circuits. "Attentive recognition," Bergson explains, "is a *circuit* in which the external object yields to us deeper and deeper parts of itself, as our memory adopts a correspondingly higher degree of tension in order to project recollections towards it."[50] It is not a matter of taking up Bergson's analysis in detail here, but only of remarking that this "symmetry" among ideas merges with the analogical work of sympathy.

This search for symmetry in effect consists in going back to an intention situated "behind" the external object, so as to constitute its interiority. But there again, this work of analogy is preceded by the ensemble of intuitive acts that slides vertically, if one may say, so as to determine the "height" at which the symmetry must be established. This work of intuition then allows for projection toward the external object and to coil up in it a "virtual object" that comes to cover it over and determine its sense. The work of analogy properly so called is thereby accomplished. What is the virtual object situated behind the object if not, in reality, its virtual subject, that is to say, its consciousness, intention, or direction? The circuit of recognition goes from idea to idea, following a symmetry, a spiritual work of analogy. Analogy is memory throughout. We recognize the other in us, and this allows us to recognize ourselves in the other.

In the passage cited, it is not only a question of recognition but also of sense. From this point of view, it is not excessive to say that all of Bergson's texts that are devoted to recognition are equally texts devoted to the ideality of sense. "Recognize" means to simultaneously understand and interpret. In this sense, memory is mind. From this point of view, it has never been sufficiently emphasized, even in the most detailed of analyses devoted to it, that *Matter and Memory* is a book that is entirely devoted to the question of sense in the same way as are the contemporaneous attempts of Frege, Husserl, and Meinong. Of course, as the book's subtitle indicates, the book bears on the "relation of mind and body," that is to say on perception, as it is through perception that the relation occurs. But perception in turn is explained by two distinct forms of memory. On the one hand is contraction-memory, the function of which is to *qualify* material movements—that is to say, to contract the innumerable vibrations of matter into qualities. "Our memory solidifies into sensible qualities the continuous flow of things."[51] On the other hand is recollection-memory, which has as its function to *signify* the spiritual movements that are actualized in matter, here sonorous matter. We said so earlier: the leap into the past is equally a leap into the element of sense in general because in reality it is a matter of one and the same thing.[52] The theory of recollection-memory must be read in parallel as a theory of sense and signification. In any case, if Bergson can criticize language as an instrument of arbitrary cutting out, it is because with recollection-memory he already has at his disposal a theory of sense that is relatively free of the spatialities of language.

Thus the mind can accompany the apparent discontinuities of language, as it doesn't stop reestablishing the ideal or spiritual continuity, of which language use is the actualization, on another plane: "I can indeed understand your speech if I start from a thought analogous to your own and follow its windings with the aid of verbal images which are so many signposts that show me the way from time to time."[53] Again, everything is an affair of movement. On the one hand, the locutor progresses horizontally, so to speak, according to the linkage of his utterances; on the other, the auditor moves vertically, trying each time to grasp the source on the basis of which the locutor is producing his utterances. He projects behind the succession of these utterances a changing "virtual object" that constitutes the sense from which the signification of the ensemble derives. But this virtual object becomes "subject" or "tendency" to the extent that it gives a direction or expresses an intention. Intention here is not at all confused with the explicit intention of the locutor but with a more profound vital or spiritual "tonality."[54] Recognition of the intention is not based on what the locutor says but that from which what makes him speak flows: his source, or the "more and more distant conditions with which [his utterance] forms one system."[55] One doesn't look toward the utterances but toward the "dispositions" from which they derive. The whole of this process of projection constitutes analogical reasoning insofar as it relates movements to a common "idea" or a "tonal" level—in short, to the same level of spiritual tension.

One can see that analogical reasoning necessarily has affective underpinnings. Tonality must not just be understood as the level of sense that one must reach but also as the vital tonality that we vibrate with internally so as to reach this level of sense. In other words, the closed circuit of deepening that Bergson describes in *Matter and Memory* is inseparable, at a deeper level, from vibrations open onto other realities. At this level, we are nothing more than vibration, a certain tonal level that endures. This is our very essence. It is from this vibration that one can open up onto other realities and enter into their point of view, insofar as one succeeds in adjusting the vibrations of two instruments so they are in tune with each other. There is certainly no preestablished harmony in Bergson, but there is a synchronization that is always in the making—or unmaking—between distinct rhythms of duration, which the intellectual form of analogical reasoning testifies to. Knowing, for Bergson, is always to enter into a movement, like one is moved by a melody or like one enters into a dance. One should speak of perspectivism in this sense. There is something deeper than our intelligence, deeper even than our affective or emotional life: the particular rhythm of duration by which we enter into relation with other realities. "Others delve yet deeper still. Beneath these joys and sorrows which can, at a pinch, be translated into a language, they grasp something that is common with language, certain rhythms of life and breath that are closer to man this his inmost feelings, being the living law—varying with each individual—of his enthusiasm and despair, his hopes and regrets. By setting free and emphasizing this music, they force it upon our attention; they compel us, willy-nilly, to fall in with it, like passers-by who join in a dance. And they impel us to set in motion, in the depths of our being, some secret chord which was only waiting to thrill."[56]

This set of remarks leads us back, finally, to the general element of duration and to Bergson's monism. We know that with *Duration and Simultaneity* Bergson starts to develop the hypothesis of a single Duration, a universal Time inside which the variable "fluxes" or durations coexist. But how does Bergson come to construct such a monism? The coexistence of durations is only possible by virtue of their integration on the inside of a duration that contains them. That is the sense of Deleuze's explanation of this point: "Two fluxes could never be said to be coexistent or simultaneous if they were not contained in a third one. The flight of the bird and my own duration are only simultaneous insofar as my own duration divides in two and is reflected in another that contains it at the same time as it contains the flight of the bird. [. . .] It is in this sense that my duration essentially has the power to disclose other durations, to encompass the others and to encompass itself ad infinitum."[57] Deleuze makes it clear that this single duration does not divide into itself without changing nature—hence the possibility of a division of fluxes into so many distinct durations.

But this should be completed. Duration in effect would not encompass itself, extracting what is common from between the fluxes, if there wasn't an analogical reasoning established first. It is a matter of a "barely conscious" reasoning, Bergson says, but that is what allows a monism of time to be thought. "They are really multiple consciousnesses sprung from ours, similar to ours, that we entrust with forging a chain across the immensity of the universe and with attesting, through the identity of their inner durations and the contiguity of their outer experiences, the singleness of an impersonal Time."[58] Thus only intuition can bring me into contact with durations other than my own, because it reveals to me that I am not just inner duration but also élan vital, material movement, voluntary effort, or personal vocation, but only sympathy can propagate or project this alterity throughout the entire universe so as to grasp it paradoxically in a monism that testifies to the prodigious plasticity of the mind and of the extension of its circuits of recognition. The mind is not all; it is not the whole but it is the analog, the sympathizer of the whole, insofar as it has the strength to be moved by all the movements that compose the universe. In every regard, the affect of sympathy really does appear as the indispensable complement of intuition.

It is by sympathy that life and matter become consciousness, but by intuition that the mind discovers itself to be duration. Of memory, one can say that it is consciousness become duration (intuition), just as easily as one can say that it is duration become consciousness (sympathy), on condition that one doesn't confuse the two operations. Certainly intuition comes first, but it receives from sympathy the extension that allows it to become a general method. One thus understands what Bergson means when he sees in sympathy the means for passing to the interior of realities. It is also the means by which a philosophy in conformity with intuition can be deployed. One can even say that sympathy gives access to the essence of each totality considered: mobility of the material, élan of the vital, obligation of the social, and aspiration of the personal. However, the leap of thought into duration is needed first in order to deploy this access to essences. In other words, sympathy receives from intuition its condition, whereas intuition receives from sympathy its extension and its generality. It is through sympathy, and only through sympathy, that all the artifice and all the efficacity of the Bergsonian method is deployed.

The Attachment
to Life

Bergson the Doctor
of Civilization

> Attachment and detachment: these are the two
> poles between which morality oscillates.
> —*Bergson*

Readers of Bergson are familiar with a concept that first appears in *Matter and Memory* and that he rediscovers subsequently spread throughout his work. It is a matter of the concept of "attention to life."[1] In the foreword to *Matter and Memory*, rewritten in 1911, Bergson comes back expressly to this concept and declares "our psychic life may be lived at different heights [. . .] according to the degree of our attention to life. Here we have one of the ruling ideas of this book."[2] This tells us the decisive importance that Bergson accords to this concept, and we understand why. Attention to life effectively designates the mechanism through which we do not stop adapting to the demands of the world in which we live; it is defined as the "sense of the real."[3] Bergson invokes it to account for our constant effort at conscious and unconscious adjustment to the "reality" of each situation. If this concept occupies a central place [in Bergson's work], it is because it allows a dividing line to be traced between the normal and the pathological that strictly intersects the distinction between the real and the unreal (dream, *délire*[4]), but also because it is the point on which the entirety of the deductive movement that animates *Matter and*

Memory converges. Attention to life is the ultimate consequence, the point of equilibrium where the whole of matter and the whole of memory meet up. This equilibrium assures us of a normal life, but [only] because it doesn't stop struggling against the disequilibria that can makes us fall into a pathological life at each instant.

But there is another concept, which only appears in the *Two Sources*, and that is the concept of attachment to life. If until now it has not really been studied for itself, this is doubtless because it has been seen as a simple variant or prolonging of attention to life. However, it is evident that not only does attachment to life play an entirely distinct role in the *Two Sources* to that of attention to life in *Matter and Memory*, but that it nevertheless also plays a role there that is just as crucial. It effectively allows a new type of equilibrium to be described, a new type of vitality, and, correlatively, a new type of pathology. It is true that in appearance the problems encountered by Bergson concern above all sociology and ethnology, as well as the history of religions and civilizations. But if that is indeed where the problems are encountered, it is not at this level that they are posed. They can only be grasped adequately at the level of tendencies, conceived as Nature and Life.

The plane of Nature is in effect constituted as "dispositions" that make man a social animal: the tendency to obey, believe, and tell stories. These dispositions circumscribe the circle in which man deploys the forms of his humanity. These tendencies all respond to the same vital imperative: to shake off the depressing power of the intelligence. Through its representations, the intelligence effectively has the power to "slow down the movement of life in man."[5] More precisely, it undoes the links that attach man to life. It is not a matter here of individual depression but of a "biological" depression that afflicts the species in its entirety. Man, an intelligent being, is defined as a sick species. The general problem around which the *Two Sources* is constructed follows on from this displacement of the dividing line between the normal and the pathological: how can man overcome this illness even though it constitutes him as a species? What are the means that life invents so as to surmount this depression provoked by the representations of the intelligence? In other words, how does man become attached to life? Is he even still attached to it?[6] After Nietzsche, although in an entirely different manner and with entirely different responses, Bergson discovers that depression is the major affair of morality and of religion insofar as they constitute precisely two essential forms of attachment to life.

Let us return for a moment to attention to life. It is not a matter of an attention of a psychological order but a biological order inherent to the species; it is defined as a faculty for anticipation of and adaptation to the demands of the present moment—adaptation because it is a matter of responding to the demands of the present moment, and anticipation because one only takes an interest in the present moment in view of the immediate future. To adapt is to anticipate. Attention to life submits our relation with the external world to a schema of question/answer. On the one hand, the present poses a question to our sensorimotor activity; on the other, memory provides a precise response that clarifies the immediate future in the form of an action to be carried out. Everything takes places as if the (social, material) world never stopped asking us: and what is to be done now? "On the one hand, the sensori-motor state [. . .] delineates the present direction of memory, being nothing else, in fact, than its actual and acting extremity; and, on the other hand, this memory itself, with the totality of our past, is continually pressing forward, so as to insert the largest possible part of itself into the present action."[7] Attention to life is characterized by a quasi-constant tension that interests us in the external world and obliges us to respond to its incessant imperatives.

This tension characterizes the situation of a balanced life, inasmuch as it maintains a solidarity between our psychological life and our motor activity. Our intellectual equilibrium rests entirely on the structure of these sensorimotor apparatuses, insofar as they fix the mind or constrain it to being interested in external life. Of course, certain humans, such as artists and philosophers, who guide us to a more complete perception of reality, live with a relative inattention to life. They turn aside our attention "from the part of the universe which interests us from a practical viewpoint and *turn it back* toward what serves no practical purpose,"[8] and a momentary displacement of our equilibrium results from it. But in a general manner, it is from the body— from the brain—that intelligence receives the ballast for its equilibrium and its capacity for adjustment to the demands of the material world. That is why attention to life is correlatively defined as the "sense of the real."[9] Any relaxation of this tension results in the individual breaking contact with the real, thus becoming disinterested. "Relax this tension or destroy this equilibrium: everything happens as if attention detached itself from life."[10] If the relaxation of tension is observed in all cases of distraction (dreaming, hypnotic fixation, automatisms), then the rupture of equilibrium is observed in all cases of mental pathology (aphasia, psychasthenia), when the mind is no longer fixed by the sensorimotor montages of the body and loses its way. As in [the work of Pierre] Janet, mental pathologies are characterized by a loss of the sense of the real; things perceived are "less ballasted, less solidly directed towards the real," and the mind falls into psychosis. [11] What is opposed to this psychosis is a normality that is confused with the intellectual equilibrium of good sense. With this schema, Bergson has available to him a general framework that allows him to determine the relations of the normal and the pathological. The normal is the ensemble of pathologies that are prevented, warded off, counterbalanced by the sensorimotor adaptation of our body to the external world. At this level, the normal is, in sum, nothing but pathology prevented.[12]

At an entirely different level, one can recognize here

the general principles of contraction and relaxation that are exercised throughout the universe and that define its different levels. The human species appears at one of these levels, with the degree of tension that is proper to it. Depending on the degrees of relaxation of this tension, its distraction makes it fall momentarily into dreaming or to sink definitively into mental illness. But there is another distraction, which is neither variable nor accidental and which concerns the species in its entirety: that of man as intelligent being. The intelligence is precisely what distracts man from life itself; it is a form of inattention to life. The pure intelligence is in effect characterized by a "natural inability to comprehend life"[13] insofar as it always perceives life from the outside. The intelligence is life having become external to itself.

Man only perceives life through the forms by which his intelligence represents it to him. As in Plotinus, he allows himself to be hypnotized by these forms without being able to break the spell—the victim of a sort of morbid narcissism. Matter is often invoked as what interrupts or at least slows down the creative evolution of the élan vital. Perhaps it is form that, in man, is the most powerful motive for interruption, a sort of death in life, in which "the letter kills the spirit."[14] So much is this the case that the human species, like the other species, lives imprisoned in a circle. "From the bottom to the top of the organized world we do indeed find one great effort; but most often, this effort turns short, sometimes paralyzed by contrary forces, sometimes diverted from what it should do by what it does, absorbed by the form it is engaged in taking, hypnotized as it is by a mirror."[15] Beyond the prodigious breakthrough that the intelligence represents for the élan vital, Bergson perceives in it the sign of a profound relaxing, the symptom of a loss of vitality, as his capacity to adapt to the material world testifies. This capacity effectively consists of aligning oneself with the movement of relaxation that for its part follows the material world. "What appears from the point of view of the intelligence as an effort, is in itself a letting go."[16] The breakthrough of the intelligence is translated on this level by a veritable *vital deficit* that is constitutive of its very normality.[17]

In *Creative Evolution*, the problem that this loss of vitality of the human species poses is not tackled in its own right; it is not considered a problem that it is the task of humanity to solve, but as the solution to a problem posed by the élan vital. It is only examined from the double point of view of a "theory of life" and a "theory of knowledge." It is with the *Two Sources* that the problem is really posed: how can humanity compensates for this defect? How can it counterbalance the perturbing effects of the intelligence, the disequilibrium that threatens it as a species?[18] That is the central problem of the book. The problem is biological, anthropological, social, or political, depending on the level at which one situates it. However, it is relative to neither the social world nor to the history of religions or civilizations. Societies and religions are only the fields within which the problem is finally actualized. Once again, if that is where the problem is encountered, then it is not at this level that the problem is posed.

We know how Bergson describes this vital deficit in the *Two Sources*. Considered in itself, the intelligence is characterized by a triple power of dissolution, depression, and discouragement: it dissolves the link that attaches man to other men (by the representation of his personal interest); it depresses his élan vital (by the representation of the ineluctability of death); finally, it discourages his power of acting (by the representation of a margin of the unexpected).[19] What testifies to this loss of vitality is not only the content of these representations but also the very fact of representation, insofar as it manifests an interruption of the élan, which instinctively leads living beings to act. That the intelligence proceeds through representation is already the sign of a lack of vitality. What the contents of representation testify to in turn is an indifference toward life, which flows from this very deficit. If the intelligence allows for a greater adaptation to the demands of the material world, then it is on the background of a vital depression that renders it possible.

Except that to live, it is not enough just to adapt. One must in the first place be attached to life. Reduced purely to his intelligence, man would never have constituted a viable species if nature had not found the means of counterbalancing this equilibrium in attaching him to life. Is that not precisely the central thesis of the *Two Sources*? Is it not by this general notion of the "attachment to life" that all the new concepts introduced in the *Two Sources* (the whole of obligation, the storytelling function, closed society, open society, creative emotion) are animated? One can see this initially when Bergson describes the "whole of obligation." Obligation is effectively presented as the means that nature has found to attach everyone's self to society, and thereby to oneself. Obligation in this sense acts as a point of attachment: "It is on the surface, at the point where it inserts itself into the close-woven tissue of other exteriorized personalities, that our ego generally finds its point of attachment; its solidity lies in this solidarity. But, at the point where it is attached, it is itself socialized. Obligation, which we look upon as a bond between men, first binds us to ourselves."[20] At this level, the attachment to life is indirect, as it passes via the attachment to others (the family, the state, the nation), but already it has the effect of counterbalancing the dissolution of the social link that the intelligence provokes. One might object that it is a matter of an attachment to society and not to life itself, but that would be to forget that for Bergson, the social is of a vital order, as the fact that obligation responds to a virtual instinct, to an "intention" of nature,[21] testifies. It would also be to forget that attachment to others is an attachment to oneself in the form of a "social self" that is constituted in interaction with others.

However, the attachment to life takes another form when Bergson examines the social role of religions by means of his description of the storytelling function. We know that the creation of this concept has to provide a reason for the fact of religion ("there has never been a society without religion"[22]) but also for the fact of their absurdity ("what a farrago of error and folly!"[23]). But religion in turn must provide a reason for the storytelling function: "Standing to religion in the relationship of effect and not of cause."[24] Religion produces the storytelling function at the same time as storytelling produces religions. There is nothing circular about the explanation, provided that one distinguishes between two senses of the word "religion." In the first sense, it is a matter of the religions effectively imagined by historically determined civilizations (such as Judaism, Buddhism, and Christianity). That is what the storytelling function explains by its power of imagination. Religions are effectively explained by our capacity for world delirium, to project onto it invisible, active powers.

One still has to explain how, in this precise case, delirium translates a vital need of the species. Hence a second sense, according to which "religion" no longer designates a determinate dogma but a simple and original act: the act of believing. According to this second sense, religion is defined as an "original tendency,"[25] a vital requirement. We have a vital need to believe. Without a doubt, even the act of believing responds to a structure of our biological organization.[26] We are naturally religious, although none of our religions is natural. What constitutes our natural religiosity are two acts: belief and delusion [*délire*]. But delusion is only vital if it is determined by the act of believing.[27] If we become delirious [*nous délirons*], it is first so as to believe. That is why our fabulations must be inserted into the world in order to be made real. One tells stories to the extent that imaginary or delirious representations can pass themselves off as real—the very definition of belief. To believe is to take something to be real. This signifies that these phantasmic representations acquire the same sensorimotor effectiveness as the representations of the real according to which we customarily act. Man inserts his fables into the real world, but also envelops the real world in his fables.

What vital function does belief have for the human species? Why does man need religious delusion [*délire*]? "Religion is that element which, in beings endowed with reason, is called upon to make good any deficiency of attachment to life."[28] After obedience, belief constitutes the second form of attachment to life. "Static religion, such as we find it when it stands alone, attaches man to life, and consequently the individual to society, by telling him tales on a par with those with which we lull children to sleep."[29] To live, we must become delirious about [*délirer*] the world, project onto it outlines of personality, superior powers, transcendent beings. In short, we must fabulate religions. Under the impulse of instinct, the intelligence effectively confers on significant events a unity and an individuality that makes of each one "a mischievous, maybe a malignant, being, but still one of ourselves, with something sociable and human about it."[30] Behind natural phenomena, one first projects "intentions" that are quickly transformed into independent entities ("spirits") and that finally form complete divinities, composing the whole of a religion. What attaches us to life is no longer the whole of obligation but the whole of religion as belief. It is no longer the act of obeying but rather the act of believing. This second form of attachment is nevertheless constructed on the same model as the first. Attachment to life remains inseparable from attachment to a group, except that this group now merges with a society of "phantasmic beings" that live a life akin to our own, one in solidarity with our own but higher than our own.[31]

Correlatively, one can measure everything that separates the notion of attachment to life from that of attention to life. On the one hand, the function of attention to life is to prevent delusion [*délire*]; on the other, attachment to life renders such delusion [*délire*] indispensable. In the first case, the "sense of the real" allows a possible mental disequilibrium to be warded off; in the second case, storytelling as the sense of the unreal allows the disequilibria into which the intelligence would drag the species to be counterbalanced: "We postulate a certain instinctive activity; then, calling into play intelligence, we try to discover whether it leads to a dangerous disturbance; if it does, the balance will probably be restored through representations evoked by instinct within the disturbing intelligence; if such representations exist, they are elementary religious ideas."[32] What is properly vital in belief (that is, the interpolating of imaginary representations into the chains of representations of the real by the intelligence[33]) is the restoring of a "natural equilibrium" that the intelligence disturbs.[34]

How do beliefs go about attaching us to life? In what way do these fabulations attach us to life? They compensate the vital deficit of the species by increasing its sentiment of confidence. As Bergson says, "In default of power, we must have confidence."[35] Belief is for confidence; that is its vital function. "[The archer] draws his bow and takes his aim; but his thought inclines rather towards the extra-mechanical cause which is to direct the arrow where it should go, because, failing the weapon which would make him sure of hitting the mark, his faith in causality will give him the self-confidence which enables him to take better aim."[36] If man lacks confidence, it is because his intelligence represents an order of reality to him that threatens his existence and his individual power to act (the margin of unpredictability, ineluctable death). In what way does the fact of projecting into the real world fictitious entities or personalities favor confidence? It is because these projections acknowledge a place for him: man is now observed, helped, supported, like children are. For confidence to be established, it is not enough to project humanity everywhere. This humanity must also turn toward man and assist or reject him—in short, offer him a privileged place.

The intelligence offers a representation of an order that excludes us or which contests the place that we occupy: the unavoidable death and margin of unpredictability that thwart our projects. We occupy only one place among many in world that has a determinate order. From this point of view, there is no difference between representing to oneself a world full of the unforeseen, like the primitive intelligence does, and representing to oneself a totally predictable world, like the scientific intelligence does. In both cases, it is a matter of a world that contests the importance of our situation. What belief fabulates is a privileged place. This privileged place is the center. Storytelling places us at the center of the world to the extent that the ensemble of forces of nature is organized *for* us. Religious anthropomorphism is anthropocentric. "For, look at any other animal. [. . .] Does it actually believe itself to be the centre of the world? Probably not, for it has no conception of the world as such, and, besides, it has not the slightest inclination to speculate. But [. . .] it obviously behaves as though everything in nature were combined solely with a view to its well-being and in the interest of its species. Such is its conviction, not intellectualized, but lived, a conviction which sustains the animal and is indistinguishable from its effort to live. You bring reflection into play, however, and this conviction will vanish; man will perceive himself, will think of himself, as a speck in the immensity of the universe. He would feel lost, if the effort to live did not at once project into his intelligence, into the very place that this perception and this reflection were about to occupy, the opposing image of things and events turning towards man; whether well disposed or ill disposed, a certain intention of his environment follows him then everywhere, just as the moon seems to run with him when he runs."[37] In other words, confidence is the way in which the world reflects an exceptional place for man, the way in which he feels himself taken into consideration, says Bergson. It transforms an indifferent world into a veritable milieu, an *Umwelt*.

These two forms of attachment to life (obedience and belief) circumscribe the limits of the human species. Intelligence, obedience, and belief are the three faculties that fix these limits at the same time as they determine the humanity in man. The history of science and of techniques, the history of societies, and the history of religions are the three histories of humanity; they are the history of the respective progress of each faculty within the circle in which the human species turns. As a species, man lives within these circles. Certainly he can enlarge them, but he cannot break them. He cannot raise himself above his intelligence; nor can he leap beyond himself so as to attain the superhuman. At this level, religion remains a static religion: it enlarges a circle or a series of circles that it does not manage to escape.[38] They are like spheres or bubbles of humanity that are confused with the scientific, technical, territorial, and religious conquests of the globe; they are closed societies. Bergson doesn't stop repeating that one doesn't get out of the closed loop, out of this turning around of the human species on itself by an effort of the same nature as that by which one surmounts the depressing power of the intelligence. With static religion, one doesn't escape from the sickness of the species; one only makes it livable. For Bergson, as for Nietzsche, the real sickness is not being sick but when the means that one has for escaping from the sickness are still a part of the sickness and testify to the impossibility of escaping it.[39]

What sickness does man suffer from? What is the general diagnosis of the *Two Sources*? It is no longer a matter of a sickness that is likely to threaten his normality. It is no longer a matter of the risks of psychoses that his attention to life, at the cost of a constant tension, protect him from. His sickness is his very normality. What he suffers from is from his intelligence and the "representations of the real" that it forces on his attention. He can only bear them on condition that he brings delusion [*délire*], fabulations that restore his attachment to life and reconstitute his "natural equilibrium,"[40] into them. But he thereby remains subject to his intelligence. He doesn't liberate himself from his submissiveness; he only renders it bearable. This equilibrium is made merely from the compensations, even the consolations, that characterize the sickness from which he cannot escape: his neurosis. This neurosis is doubtless always on the point of collapsing into psychosis. Doesn't Bergson in effect say that societies live in a sort of permanent dream or nightmare?[41] The human species is a neurosis of life [itself]; it is life neuroticized—that is the diagnosis of the *Two Sources*. We know that since *Matter and Memory*, man is virtually psychotic, but we learn with the *Two Sources* that he is actually, specifically, effectively neuroticized, as those fabulations of his destined to console him for his "representation of reality," and which he "clings" onto in an infantile manner testify.[42]

To escape from his sickness—which defines his normality too as well—it is necessary for man to leap outside of his intelligence and over his humanity. That is what happens with the mystic, through whom Bergson supposes a more-than-human man is aimed at.[43] "Why should man not recover the confidence he lacks [*since he seeks it outside*], or which has perhaps been undermined by reflection, by turning back for fresh impetus [*élan*], in the direction whence that impetus [*élan*] came? Not through intelligence, at least not through intelligence alone, could he do so [. . .] joy in joy, love of that which is all love. [. . .] Now detachment from each particular thing would become attachment to life in general."[44] There is a third form of attachment to life. But why does Bergson immediately define it by detachment? Because one is now attached to the very movements of life and no longer to the forms by which we think them, by which we deform them so as to make of them the fixed and permanent beings that we love. This is what Bergson detects in maternal love, which isn't primarily love for a being but for the movement of life that passes from mother to child, which is transmitted from one to the other. This love "shows us each generation leaning over the generation that shall follow. It allows us a glimpse of the fact that the living being is above all a thoroughfare and that the essence of life is in the movement by which life is transmitted."[45] It is no longer a matter of a morbid narcissism, of an intelligence in love with the circles in which it turns, but rather the matter of a vital narcissism.

We are no longer attached to beings but to that which is movement in them—nothing but movement. As Bergson already said in *Creative Evolution*, "In order that our consciousness shall coincide with something of its principle, it must detach itself from the *already-made* and attach itself to the *being-made*. It needs that, turning back on itself and twisting on itself, the faculty of *seeing* should be made to be one with the act of willing, a painful effort which we can make suddenly, doing violence to our nature, but cannot sustain more than a few moments."[46] By the subterranean play of affects, our intelligence attached itself to forms and to beings that it cut out from and then fixed in the continuous movement of things. The false metaphysical problems of being and of nothingness follow from it as epistemological figures of attachment. The fictions of religion follow from it too, but this time as anthropological figures of attachment. Only the effort at relying on the immanence of movement and duration can protect us from the transcendences of metaphysics and religion.

If we have to do violence to nature to achieve such detachment, it is because attachment to life (or confidence) changes nature. It is precisely the mystic who leaps beyond the plane of Nature, that is to say, outside the circles in which his belonging to the species kept him.[47] He even begins to constitute a species all of his own.[48] One is no longer dealing with an extensive enlargement or a qualitative increase, but rather with an intensive leap that merges with a movement of conversion.[49] But as long as one doesn't describe the effective process by which this leap is accomplished, this remains abstract or allusive. One understands that Bergson can describe it as an abnormal—albeit nonpathological—process[50] because it is effectively a matter of freeing oneself up from the normality of the species, which is one with the sickness that otherwise characterizes it. "The truth is that these abnormal states, resembling morbid

72

states, and sometimes doubtless very akin to them, are easily comprehensible, if we only stop to think what a shock to the soul is the passing from the static to the dynamic, from the closed to the open, from everyday life to mystic life. When the darkest depths of the soul are stirred, what rises to the surface and attains consciousness takes on there, if it be intense enough, the form of an image or an emotion. [. . .] But they both may express the fact that the disturbance is a systematic readjustment with a view to equilibrium on a higher level."[51] One only escapes from the neurosis proper to the human species by a sort of psychotic experience (ecstasies, hallucinations, raptures), a schizophrenic episode that leads us to a health beyond the normal, a new norm of life characterized by a "superior equilibrium."

To understand what this equilibrium consists of, one must take a detour and briefly set out the profound theory of equilibria that runs through the whole of Bergsonism. In a sense, Bergson thinks of everything in terms of equilibria and ruptures of equilibria. It is first the equilibrium of the material world, of which all the possible parts reciprocally hinder each other from standing out.[52] But this equilibrium is quickly broken with the appearance of living bodies, whose indetermination testifies to a constant disequilibrium between action undergone and action executed. In its turn, the élan vital has to find an equilibrium that counterbalances the disequilibrium that is provoked by the actualization of each of the tendencies it is heavy with. This equilibrium is found when one tendency manages to subordinate the others, at the same time as the latter must prevent the former from provoking a new disequilibrium. In this sense, each mixture that Bergson extracts describes an equilibrium among tendencies that, taken by themselves, are always factors of disequilibrium. Each mixture thus appears as a modus vivendi.[53] Each level is defined by an equilibrium that is determinate but full of disequilibria that testify to the existence of other levels. Thus we have seen that at the heart of the human species an *intellectual* equilibrium is first established, which makes of man a sort of modus vivendi between the impulsive man of action and the contemplative dreamer.[54] Subsequently a *natural* equilibrium is established between the intelligence and the "virtual instincts" of obedience and belief, which form a counterweight to it. This is a second normality of a social order that makes of man a being who doesn't act without obeying mechanically and who doesn't think without believing religiously. Each one of these two equilibria forms a definite system—a system of intellectual life in one case and a system of social life in the other.

Finally, beyond these two forms of normality, a "superior equilibrium" that is vital or spiritual is established, the functioning of which must be defined. As Bergson says, it presupposes a "systematic rearrangement." Here Bergson appears rather allusive. But perhaps these allusions are sufficient to indicate what new system is put in place and what new type of attachment to life it supposes and engenders. The intensive leap, Bergson makes clear, upsets the "regular relations of the conscious to the unconscious."[55] One passes from the intellectual and social self to the "fundamental self"—the same fundamental self as was already described in *Time and Freewill*. How are these two selves distinguished from the point of view of their respective systems? In the first case, attention to life is determined by the sensorimotor montages that enable it to respond to the variety of situations encountered. The appeal or question that determines memory to present the appropriate responses comes from the perception of the present situation, insofar as the body finds itself inserted in it.[56] One rediscovers the imperative character of the present as an incessant "now!" We have in effect seen that attention to life presented itself above all as question/answer system. It is the same system that one rediscovers in the first forms of attachment to life, except that the questions no longer emanate directly from the present situation; they are reflected by the intelligence, which projects them into the future. This is the future to which our social obligations and religious beliefs respond. Responding to the future is even the essential function of static religion.

The intensive leap that Bergson describes upsets the entirety of this system, at the cost of a profound loss of equilibrium, which mystic crises testify to. The imperative no longer emanates either from the present or from its reflection in the future; it emanates from the past—the deepest past, an immemorial past, which we have seen constitutes a sort of memory of the future. "Shaken to its depths by the current which is about to sweep it forward, the soul ceases to revolve around itself. [. . .] It stops, as though to listen to a voice calling. Then it lets itself go, straight onward."[57] What is this voice if not an imperative that emanates from memory or from the élan vital like a spiritual force?[58] It is memory that from within itself launches a response, to which man as a whole responses. One is now dealing with a response/response system.[59] It is the totality of the past that, in the manner of a *vocatio*, passes into action, as a function of its own demands, and no longer of material, personal, and social demands. This appeal is an "imperative demand for creation."[60] After obeying and believing, *creating* is the third verb of the *Two Sources*, the third imperative. But in reality this imperative testifies to a liberation; for the mystic, nothing will be an obstacle to the power of creation any longer. "Effort remains indispensible, endurance and perseverance likewise. But they come of themselves, they develop of their own accord, in a soul acting and acted upon"[61] to the point that the resistances of matter seem to give way under it impulsion "just as a punster might thank the words he comes across for lending themselves to his fun."[62] It remains to be determined from whence this imperative draws its eruptive force, able to upset existing systems and free up man from the circles in which nature imprisons him.

We can say that it is a question of life or of the élan vital insofar as it acts at a deeper level than that of nature, as if naturing nature and natured nature were not situated on the same plane.[63] But posed in this way, the response remains abstract. We can say that the effort that is produced now coincides with its principle, but then the response is too theoretical, even if the principle is conceived as an active force and not as a logical necessity. What allows the principle to act with this power still has to be determined, what allows it to force nature so as to liberate such considerable creative energy. As we have seen, one can only understand it if the point to which this élan is constrained and as if choked is measured. It is in this choking off that the élan is filled with all its future explosive force: "An activity of a superior kind, which to be operative requires one of a lower order, must call forth this activity, or at least permit it to function, if necessary, even at the cost of having to defend itself against it; experience shows that if, in the case of two contrary but complementary tendencies, we find one to have grown until it tries to monopolize all the room, the other will profit by this, provided it has been able to survive; its turn will come again, and it will then benefit by everything which has been done without its aid, which has even been energetically developed in specific *opposition* to it."[64] Everything happens as if human equilibrium, as if the normality engendered by this equilibrium, ceased to be viable; at a deeper level, it is perceived and lived as a disequilibrium, insofar as its modus vivendi doesn't stop repressing the creative forces at the heart of the individual.

As we have seen, the accumulation of all this coercion—all this sometimes imperceptible repression—is condensed in an act of revolt, an intensive leap or explosive act.[65] That is what Bergson designates by the term "creative emotion." So what is creative emotion? Creative emotion designates the integral of all the affections of sensibility that precede the intelligence and that the intelligence can only repress, as it is attached not to the affective states of subjects but to the objects around which these states crystallize. Such is the natural tendency of the intelligence. Consequently it separates from the emotion that bears it; it represses its "organic development" so as to substitute for it the logical order of its representations.[66] One follows nothing but the effect that emotion produces through its crystallization in the object; one follows the objects through the representation of effects that one can expect from it, independent of any emotion. At this level, emotion always appears as second, an effect and not a cause. Inversely, one can speak of creative emotion when it engenders the objects that correspond to it and express it. These objects then become "real inventions, comparable to those of the musician. [. . .] Thus mountains may, since the beginning of time, have had the faculty of rousing in those who looked upon them certain feelings comparable with sensations, and indeed inseparable from the mountains. But Rousseau created in connection with them a new and original emotion."[67] It is no longer the object that provokes a determinate emotion but on the contrary the emotion that engenders its object, returned to its supra- or subrepresentative nonhuman characteristics. There is something of this tendency every time that one experiences a new affect, a tremendous emotion, of a metaphysical, ethical, or aesthetic order.

Of course, these emotions and these affects only touch us through the matter that expresses them. Creation is doubtless never as elevated as the demand that carries it along, although it does make it felt. One rediscovers here the conclusions of *Creative Evolution*: the created never equals the demand for creation of which it is a product. Living forms are never elevated as high as what the élan vital aimed at through them. The materiality of language never manages to pull itself up to the heights of intuition—at least, this is how Bergson expresses himself most frequently. In a symbolic manner, he opposes the tension of what elevates itself with the slackening of what falls back and extends itself, as if it were a matter of two movements in contrary directions. "All our analyses show us, in life, an effort to remount the incline that matter descends."[68]

But it is well known that it is only a manner of speaking. Bergson expresses himself as if one tendency were fettered the creative effort of the other. In reality, it is their apparent antagonism that makes the creative act possible. There is no act of creation that doesn't include within itself this difference of nature or rhythm between the demand that determines it (the highest degree) and the matter in which it is actualized (the lowest degree).[69] Taken in itself, in the indivisible difference that constitutes it, the demand for creation is elevation or "rising." But its actualization—effective creation—inevitably makes it fall or drop, as it can only be actualized in a matter at a lower level. This movement is inevitable—as inevitable as expressing ideas by means of words. All creation supposes the coexistence of these two levels, which are experienced in a difference with self. All creation is a fall, and from this point of view, a failure, just as from the inverse point of view it appears as a success, taking into account the level to which it has managed to pull itself. [70] Thus, man, for example, sometimes appears as a failure (if he is compared with what would have happened if matter had not fettered the demand for creation of the élan vital to such a point) and sometimes as a success (if he is compared with other species, where consciousness has not succeeded in overcoming the resistances of matter).

It is the ensemble of these creative affects that attaches us to life. Attachment is no longer indirect, as in the previous forms. It passes neither via the society of men (the whole of obligation) nor by a society of "phantasmic beings" (the whole of religion). It is a product of life itself insofar as this latter now coincides with its creative principle. Life attaches us to it via its creative power as a creation of self by self. Attachment thus becomes love and produces joy as its essential affect. Liberated from the forms of representation, liberated from the circles in which the species turns round and round, liberated from human will, liberated from all dialectical mediation, creation no longer knows any obstacle and is thus experienced as divine. Nothing separates the demand for creation from the vital principle of the creative act itself any longer, other than their difference of level. As Bergson says, the individual acts at the same as he is "acted," as if abdicating freewill gave him access to a more powerful will. Attachment to life merges with a new form of confidence: "Let us say the henceforth for the soul there is a superabundance of life. There is a boundless impetus [élan]. There is an irresistible impulse which hurls it into vast enterprises. A calm exaltation of all its faculties makes it see things on a vast scale only, and, in spite of its own weakness, produce only what might be mightily wrought."[71]

That, at least, is what happens with the mystic, who frees himself up from any obstacle and whose power is never separated from what it is capable—hence the peaceful certainty that animates him. He doubts no longer, sure of a will that is full of itself, simultaneously an active beatitude and an acquired innocence. [72] He is thus, so to say, beyond reach, on the other side of the difference of nature, alone among men. It is completely different with the artist (or philosopher), who progresses in an anxious matter, without certainty, and asks himself whether "it will be granted to him to go on to the end."[73] He doesn't make the leap once and for all but attempts it anew each time, so as to see and to feel, to experience verticality and to traverse its levels, as if he were living astride the difference of nature that his creation itself constitutes, ceaselessly torn apart by the experiment that he makes with it, ridding himself of his humanity each time, so as to try to "realise the unrealisable."[74]

The third form of confidence or attachment to life is thus accomplished, confirming the central role that this concept plays in the *Two Sources*. The three forms of attachment that Bergson sets out correspond to the three imperatives around which the work is organized: obeying, believing, and creating as infra- or supraintellectual forces. The first two forms of attachment circumscribe closed societies and develop within the limits assigned to the human species. They form circular worlds—terrestrial as well as celestial worlds. The third form of attachment merges with the open; it is no longer stated in terms of worlds but in terms of the universe—a universe that opens up onto a plurality of worlds.[75]

After Man

Bergson
the Spiritualist

In many ways, Bergson's thinking comes after the "death of man," if one thereby understands that man has ceased to be at the center of philosophy. Man, in Bergson, is caught between levels of reality that are sometimes inferior and sometimes superior to him, making his experience, in what is properly human about it, too limited to offer any kind of interest. This is because human experience is a prisoner of circles, of all the innumerable circles that the intelligence imposes on thought and that make the human species turn around on itself.[1] Man is literally surrounded by his intelligence. If there is something that Bergson didn't stop combatting, it is these circles, precisely because they make it impossible for us to carry out the necessary leaps to change the level of reality. Thinking, for Bergson, is each time to leap out of a circle in which human experience is imprisoned. In this sense, thinking is no longer a human operation. If man, in spite of everything, retains a privileged place in Bergsonism, this is because he alone has the power, in thought, to leap beyond his intelligence and cross all the levels of reality that exceed him.

We know what makes us capable of such leaps: the spirit. In this sense, one can speak of spiritualism in Bergson, in opposition to the "intellectualism" that imprisons thought in the circles of the intelligence. But what exactly must be understood here by spiritualism? One can certainly invoke the classic definitions: explanation of the inferior by the superior; affirmation of the

81

superiority of mind over matter, against all materialism; affirmation of the independence and freedom of the mind against any form of determinism—but these are suitable for Bergson's philosophy.[2] If Bergson's spiritualism manages to avoid these too-broad definitions, it is first of all because it merges with the affirmation of a particular kind of perspectivism: to perceive with the eyes of the mind is no longer to observe from the outside, but rather to enter into another point of view, as with sympathy. Throughout his oeuvre, Bergson opposes those who have a point of view on the movement of a phenomenon and those who make movement into the point of view of the phenomenon itself, its consciousness. Thus mechanism, finalism, and evolutionism, for example, have a fixed point of view on the evolution of the species, whereas Bergson endeavors to rejoin consciousness or the internal élan of evolutionary movement—a perspective that finds itself multiplied by the divergence of evolutionary lines: the torpor of the plant, the instinct of the animal, the intelligence of man and beyond. Because everything is movement, it is every moving reality that develops its own point of view. Movement is the soul, the spirit, or the consciousness of phenomena. There is a soul of things or beings insofar as they are grasped in the pure movement that is theirs.[3] It is in this sense that Bergson can say one must "enter into what is being done . . . follow the moving reality, adopt the becoming which is the life of things."[4] From Leibniz to Nietzsche and through to Bergson and Deleuze, perspectivism has always been spiritualist, to the extent that it is a matter of extracting the spirit, the soul, the will to power, or the internal difference of such and such a reality.

If it is possible to penetrate the inside of phenomena, this means that spirit can know reality such as it is "in itself." Bergson's perspectivism thus has nothing relativistic about it, because, on the contrary, it allows an absolute knowledge to be attained: "In the absolute we live and move and have our being. The knowledge we possess of it is incomplete, no doubt, but not external or relative."[5] But as intuition is essentially reflection, it is by descending into the depth of ourselves that we reach the in-itself of things. Reality is in itself in us, to the extent that we are precisely a part of the universe and no longer a subject that is external to the objects it conceives. That means that the mind isn't just spirit but also life and matter, depending on the level of tension at which it grasps itself. Is this tension not the sign that the spirit is defined above all as a force, in the sense that it vibrates and is moved by the movements that compose the universe? It resonates with all the levels of tension of the universe, from which it extracts a "consciousness" each time. This vibration of force is the very condition of communication, with which the universe closes up on itself once again and is transformed into an object. Reciprocally, we become subjects again, incapable of escaping from our circles.

What characterizes man is the regularity of the conduct of life and thought that makes his world ordinary. Ordinary man is a tautology. Also, it is not astonishing that one only attains the life the spirit by rare, hidden entrances, which are more surreptitious and vanishing the one from the other? It is all the limit experiences that make us leap beyond ordinary human experience: déjà vu, the joy of having children, the panoramic vision of the dying, the rebellion of the free act, "pure perception"—experiences that Bergson each time reminds us of how rare and fleeting they are.[6] What world do such experiences lead to? What does the world perceived by the spirit consist of? It is a world composed uniquely of movements, in the manner of the fourth chapter of *Matter and Memory*, which describes the world of matter as a multiplicity of "numberless vibrations, all linked together in an uninterrupted continuity, all bound up with each other, and travelling in every direction like shivers through an immense body."[7] The material world is thus dematerialized, so to speak, only allowing the spiritual reality of its innumerable movements to appear. But this is also true of the world of life and the world of spirit, although tendencies and polarities are introduced here, which means that movements are no longer given over to radical immanence but are organized; they rise, fall, and reach equilibrium according to rhythms of defined durations.

This is the process of abstraction or reduction that is proper to Bergson: to grasp the movement of music independently of its melody, to grasp the movement of the mystic independently of all the voices, images, and emotions that accompany it, to grasp the current of life independent of all the created forms that it traverses, to grasp the movement of obedience and belief independently of all obligation and all religion, to grasp emotions independently of their emotional content—in short, to grasp a virtual whole independent of its always partial actualization.[8] One detaches oneself from all representation so as to rely on pure movements. One detaches oneself from qualifiers or names so as to rely on verbs. We have seen that the *Two Sources* is constructed around three verbs—to obey, to believe, to create—which constitute three essential acts of thought. But we ought to extract verbs from all of Bergson's works—to recognize, to accumulate, to explode, to fabricate, to launch, to stretch, to fall back, to flow[9]—in order to set out a sort of melodic line composed uniquely of these acts of thought that scan the rhythmic differences of duration.

Actualization, for its part, is always situated at another level; it is partial, discontinuous, and incomplete, as it cannot make the virtual whole copresent with each act pass into existence. In this sense, to actualize is always to slow down, to lag behind the movements of the spirit. The spirit always goes more quickly than man succeeds in thinking it. Is that not the very definition of man from the point of view of duration? What is a man, effectively, if not a certain rhythm of duration, or rather a plurality of rhythms of duration that are mixed up and merge with one another? Certainly, at the cost of violent efforts, man succeeds in synchronizing with other rhythms of duration, but most frequently he lags behind them and thinks everything on the basis of this delay. Man is this delay itself, an arrhythmia. He thus loses the sense of the real to the benefit of symbols, which are certainly effective but which are separate from the movement and the speed proper to this world of pure movement.

References to
Bergson's Works

CE Creative Evolution, translated by A. Mitchell (New York: Dover, 2007). Republication of 1911 Henry Holt and Co. edition.

CM The Creative Mind, translated by M. L. Andison (New York: Dover, 2007). Republication of 1946 Philosophical Library edition.

DS Duration and Simultaneity, translated by L. Jacobson (Indianapolis, Ind.: Bobbs-Merrill, 1965).

KW Key Writings, edited by K. Ansell-Pearson and J. Mullarkey (London: Continuum, 2002). This volume contains extracts from all Bergson's major writings, as well as from the *Mélanges.*

L Laughter: An Essay on the Meaning of the Comic, translated by C. Brereton and F. Rothwell (København/Los Angeles: Green Integer Books, 1999). Republication of 1911 Macmillan edition.

M Mélanges (Paris: PUF, 1972).

ME Mind-Energy, translated by H. Wildon (New York: Henry Holt and Co., 1920).

MM Matter and Memory, translated by N. M. Paul and W. S. Palmer (Yew York: Zone, 1990). Republication of 1911 George Allen and Unwin Ltd. edition.

TSM The Two Sources of Morality and Religion, translated by R. A. Audra and C. Brereton (New York: Dover, 1977). Republication of 1935 Henry Holt and Co. edition.

TFW Time and Freewill, translated by F. L. Pogson (London: George Allen and Unwin Ltd., 1919).

Notes

Introduction

1. *CM*, 61: "What, really, is the intelligence? It is the human way of thinking."

2. Ibid., 163.

3. On the relations between Heidegger and Bergson, cf. C. Riquier, "La durée pure comme esquisse de la temporalité ekstatique: Heidegger, lecteur de Bergson," in *Heidegger en dialogue, 1912–1930*, ed. S. Jollivet and C. Romano (Paris: Vrin, 2009), notably 59–60. For an entirely different point of view, see V. Jankélévitch, *L'Irréversible et la nostalgie* (Paris: Flammarion, 1974).

4. *DS* [*KW*, 206].

5. *DS* [*KW*, 205].

6. *CM*, 123.

7. See the fine pages by H. Maldiney on the time of melancholy and, based on the work of linguist G. Guillaume on the aspects of time in language, his analysis of the typical formulae of the melancholic ("if only I hadn't . . . I wouldn't be where I am now"), in H. Maldiney, *Penser l'homme et la folie* (Grenoble: Millon, 2007).

8. S. Kierkergaard, *Repetition* (Princeton, N.J.: Princeton University Press, 1983), 136–37.

9. H. James, *The Beast in the Jungle* (London: Martin Secker, 1915): "The fate he had been marked for he had met with a vengeance, he had emptied the cup to the lees; he had been the man of his time, the man, to whom nothing on earth was to have happened."

10. Maldiney, *Penser l'homme et la folie*, 96.

11. *MM*, 153: "To live in the pure present, to respond to a stimulus by the immediate reaction which prolongs it, is the mark of the lower animals: the man who proceeds in this way is a man if *impulse*. But he who lives in the past for the mere

pleasure of living there, and in whom recollections emerge into the light of consciousness without any advantage for the present situation, is hardly better fitted for action: here we have no man of impulse, but a *dreamer.*"

12. Maldiney, *Penser l'homme et la folie,* 56. What is valid for the melancholic is also valid for the man who waits indefinitely. As James's character says in *The Beast in the Jungle*: "It isn't a matter as to which I can choose, I can decide for a change. [. . .] One's in the hands of one's law."

13. *TFW,* 169–70.

14. M. Proust, "Time Regained," in *Remembrance of Things Past* (London: Wordsworth, 2006) 2:1172. In "The Guermantes Way," Proust makes it clear that the whole of the Search is the history of this "invisible vocation." On the fact that the free act in Bergson is inseparable from a vocation, see *TFW,* 215.

15. *TFW,* 215.

16. *TFW,* 184.

17. G. Deleuze, *Difference and Repetition* (London: Athlone, 1994), 83–84, and the whole of the passage devoted to the second synthesis of time.

18. Deleuze, *Difference and Repetition,* 89. When Deleuze for his part looks for a time of the future, it is not to Bergson whom he turns but to Nietzsche, in his eyes the only authentic thinker of the future.

19. On the élan vital as time of the future, see C. Riquier, *Archéologie de Bergson: Temps et métaphysique* (Paris: PUF, 2009), 353 et seq.

20. See *ME,* the chapter on memory of the present and false recognition.

21. On this point, see G. Deleuze, *Bergsonism* (New York: Zone, 1988) 57.

22. See G. Deleuze, *Bergsonism,* 51 et seq. and summary on 71: "In this way a psychological unconscious, distinct from the ontological unconscious, is defined. The latter corresponds to a recollection that is pure, virtual, impassive, inactive, *in itself.* The former represents the movement of recollection in the course of actualising itself: like Leibnizian possible, recollections try to become embodied, they exert pressure to be admitted so that a full-scale repression originating in the present and an 'attention to life' are necessary to ward off use-

less or dangerous recollections." Although Deleuze talks of a passive memory, some rare passages in *MM* (256n77 and 129) suggest that memory is endowed with activity. See also *ME*, 95 and 98: "Images, however deep and far back in our memory, are not inert and indifferent. They are active and ready; they are almost attentive."

23. Deleuze, *Bergsonism*, 105.

24. Strangely, Deleuze sees in Bergsonian freedom a process that is above all of a physical order; ibid., 107.

25. See *CM*, 169: "For one does not obtain reality from an intuition [. . .] if one has not gained its confidence by a long comradeship with its superficial manifestations. And it is not a question simply of assimilating the outstanding facts; it is necessary to accumulate and fuse such an enormous mass of them that one may be assured, in this fusion, of neutralising by one another all the preconceived and premature ideas observers may have deposited unknowingly in their observations."

26. *TSM*, 253.

27. *MM*, 150: "In the fraction of a second which covers the briefest possible perception of light, billions of vibrations have taken place, of which the first is separated from the last by an interval which is enormously divided. Your perception, however instantaneous, consists then in an incalculable multitude of remembered elements; in truth, every perception is already memory. *Practically, we perceive only the past.*"

28. Ibid., chap. 2. It goes without saying that it is not explained either by habit-memory, which Bergson makes clear is barely a memory; our habits are, so to speak, without past, as the familiarity of our everyday activities, which float in a sort of constant present, testify.

29. Cf. *CE*, 115: "It is probable that life tended at the beginning to compass at one and the same time both the manufacture of the explosive and the explosion by which it is utilised [. . .] was the very nature of matter that life found confronting it on the planet, opposed to the possibility of two tendencies evolving very far together in the same organism? What is certain is that the vegetable has trended principally in the first direction and the animal in the second direction. But if from the very first, in making the explosive, nature had for object the explosion, then it is the evolution of the animal, rather

than that of the vegetable, that indicates, on the whole, the fundamental direction of life."

30. *CM*, 70.

31. See, for example, the beginning of *TFW*, the analysis of the emotion that grace acquires, which is expressed in terms of movement alone.

32. *CM*, 104.

33. Ibid., 103.

34. See ibid., 9: "Those are the ways of thinking we use in practical life; it is particularly essential to our industry that our thought should be able to lag behind reality and remain attached, when need be, to what was or to what might be, instead of being absorbed by what is. But when we go from the domain of fabrication to that of creation, when we ask ourselves the most agonising of metaphysical problems, we virtually accept an absurdity."

The Obscure Number of Duration

1. *MM*, 71, and *TFW*, 221. See also *CM*, 15: "I kept to that [direction] because I had chosen first of all to try out my method on the problem of liberty."

2. *TFW*, 96 [translation modified]. In the same passage, Bergson makes it clear that the a priori form of sensibility in Kant corresponds in reality to a sui generis act of the intelligence. In conclusion, further on, "Kant's great mistake was to take time as a homogeneous medium" (232).

3. Ibid., 75 et seq.

4. Ibid., 78.

5. Ibid., 103: "But how can [one] fail to notice that, in order to perceive a line as a line, it is necessary to take up a position outside it, to take account of the void which surrounds it, and consequently to think a space of three dimensions?"

6. Ibid., 105 (our italics). And again "we must admit that sounds *combined with one another* and acted, not by their quantity as quantity, but by the quality which their quantity *exhibited*, ie by the rhythmic organisation of the whole" (106, our italics); "we are thus compelled to admit that we have here to do with a synthesis which is, so to speak, qualitative, a gradual organisation of our successive sensations *amongst themselves*, a unity resembling that of a phrase in a melody" (111, our italics) [translation modified]. Bergson makes it

clear that if consciousness retains the states of the external world, "it is because these distinct states of the external world give rise to other states of consciousness which permeate one another *imperceptibly organise themselves* into a whole, and bind the past to the present by this very process of connexion" (121, our italics).

7. In our opinion, this is the difficulty for F. Worms in *Bergson ou les deux sens de la vie* (Paris: PUF, 2004). His analyses insist on the notion of "mental synthesis" but only to see in it an "act" of the self, at "the limits of passivity," to be sure (66), but active at the heart of its apparent passivity.

8. *TFW*, 106: "The fact is that each increase of stimulation is taken up into the preceding stimulations, and that the whole produces on us the effect of a musical phrase which is constantly on the point of ending and constantly altered in its totality by the addition of some new note."

9. Ibid., 123 (our italics), and "When I take my first walk in a town in which I am going to live, my environment produces on me two impressions at the *same time*, one of which is destined to last while the other will constantly change" (129, our italics). Here Bergson is sketching out one of the central theses of *Matter and Memory*, the formulation of which will appear again in *ME*: "As a perception is created, its memory is sketched out alongside it, like a shadow alongside a body."

10. See ibid., 128, 132–33, 165, 231.

11. Ibid., 221: "Freedom is therefore a fact, and among the facts which we observe there is none the clearer." And in *CM*, "As freedom had become for me an undoubted fact, I had to deal with it to the exclusion of almost everything else in my first book: determinism could come to terms with it the best it could: it would have to do so, as no theory can resist a fact for long."

12. *MM*, 183–85.

13. *CM*, 147: "An empiricism worthy of the name [. . .] cuts for the object a concept appropriate to the object alone, a concept one can barely say is still a concept, since it applies only to that thing."

14. On the importance of infinitesimal calculus at the time that Bergson was working on *Time and Freewill*, see J. Milet, *Bergson et le calcul infinitesimal ou la Raison et le temps* (Paris: PUF, 1974).

15. *TFW*, 133.

16. S. Maïmon, *Essai sur la philosophie transcenden-tale* (Paris: Vrin, 1989), 49–50. See the commentaries by M. Gueroult, *La Philosophie transcendentale de Salomon Maïmon* (Paris: Alcan, 1929), 59 et seq., and G. Lebrun, "Le transcendentale et son image," in *Gilles Deleuze, une vie philosophique*, ed. E. Alliez (Paris: Les Empêcheurs de penser en rond, 1998), 214–15.

17. Maïmon, *Essai sur la philosophie transcendentale*, 50.

18. Maïmon makes it clear with the help of an example: "To be able to think a line, the understanding must draw it in thought. But to be able to present a line in intuition, it must be represented as already drawn [. . .]. In intuition, the line precedes the movement of a point; in the concept, it is the in-verse, that is to say, that for the concept of line or for its ge-netic definition, the movement of a point precedes the concept of line" (ibid., 52). On the two types of knowledge, see Guer-oult, *La Philosophie transcendentale*, 60–61. It can be com-pared with Newton's formula in his treatise *Of the Quadrature of Curves*: "Lines are described and engendered, not by a jux-taposition of their parts, but by the continuous movement of points" (quoted in Milet, *Bergson et le calcul infinitesimal*, 70).

19. Maïmon, *Essai sur la philosophie transcendentale*, 51.

20. See Gueroult, *La Philosophie transcendentale*, 61. Maïmon's formulations here are close to those of Newton in his treatise *Of the Quadrature of Curves*, which, let's recall, calls the speeds of the movements that generate magnitudes *fluxions*, and the magnitudes generated by these movements *fluent*. Also recall that Maïmon wrote a text in Hebrew on physics according to Newtonian principles three years before the appearance of his *Essay*. On this point, see J.-B. Scher-rer in Maïmon, *Essai*, 10)

21. *M*, 773.

22. Ibid., 119.

23. Ibid.

24. Ibid., 120. The same criticism can be found in *CE*, 21.

25. *MM*, 182. On this point see the analysis by Q. Meil-lassoux in "Soustraction et contraction: À propos d'une re-marque de Deleuze sur Matière et mémoire," *Philosophie* 96 (2008), which rightly invokes Maïmon, *Essai*, 96 and 79.

26. *CE*, 174 [translation modified].

27. Cf. *ME*, 13: "Suppose however that at particular mo-

ments and at particular points matter shows a certain elasticity, then and there will be the opportunity for consciousness to install itself. It will have to humble itself at first; yet once installed, it will dilate, it will spread from its point of entry and not rest till it has conquered the whole, for time is at its disposal, and the slightest quantity of indetermination, by continually adding to itself, will make up as much freedom as you like." In *CE*, Bergson even specifies that if biology were to become as precise as modern mathematics (which studies the variation of functions) "it would become to the physical chemistry of organised bodies what modern mathematics has found itself to be in relation to ancient geometry." One can without difficulty conclude that a metaphysics of life would play the same role for this new biology as that if metaphysical intuition for the idea of the differential.

28. *TSM*, 23 [translation modified].

29. Compare the decisive passage in *CM*: "The most powerful method of investigation known to the mind, the infinitesimal calculus was born of that very reversal [of the normal direction of the workings of thought] [. . .] It is true that it contents itself with the pattern, being but the science of magnitudes. It is also true that it has been able to realise these marvellous applications only through the invention of certain symbols [. . .] But metaphysics, which does not aim at any application, can and for the most part ought to abstain from converting intuition into symbol. [. . .] What it will have lost with regard to science, in utility and occurrence, it will regain in scope and range." Bergson is referring here to Newton above all. As Milet reminds us, if Bergson invokes the Newtonian idea of fluxion rather than the Leibnizian idea of the differential, it is because for Newton mathematical magnitudes are now inscribed in time. Perhaps Bergson was in this respect inspired by his reading of Cournot, when the latter recalls that "the idea that Newton had, of comparing the change, or to use his language, the flowing [*fluxio*] of all magnitudes to the flowing of time, and of considering all variable magnitudes as functions of time." M. Cournot, *Traité de l'enchaînement des idées fondamentales dans les sciences et dans l'histoire* (Paris: Hachette, 1861) book 1, 62, quoted in Milet, *Bergson et le calcul infinitesimal*, 73.

30. *TFW*, 84. On Descartes's and Leibniz's conception of

number, see Y. Belaval, *Leibniz critique de Descartes*, 2nd ed. (Paris: Gallimard, 1976), chap. 4.

31. *TFW*, 79.

32. Ibid., 82.

33. Ibid., 204.

34. Ibid., 121. See also 227.

35. Ibid., 121.

36. Ibid., 127 and 86. Sensibility "had thus ascertained in its own way the succession of four strokes, but quite otherwise than by a process of addition, and without bringing in the image of a juxtaposition of distinct terms" (127).

37. Bergson explains his choice of this term in *M*, 491. One can compare this with Leibniz, who conceives potential number as a multiplicity that one can make explicit through demonstration. For the example of the "duodenary," where what is "virtual in the proposition and contained under a certain power, finds itself rendered evident or explicit by the demonstration" [translation modified], see G. W. Leibniz, "On Freedom," in *Leibniz: Philosophical Papers and Letters*, ed. L. Loemker (Chicago: Chicago University Press, 1956), §8.

38. *TFW*, 8, 14, 132: "A violent love or a deep melancholy takes possession of our soul: here we feel a thousand different elements which dissolve into and permeate one another without any precise outlines, without the least tendency to externalise themselves in relation to one another" (132).

39. Ibid., 18: "The degrees of depth [correspond] to the larger or smaller numbers of elementary psychic phenomena which we dimly discern in the fundamental emotion."

40. See G. W. Leibniz, *New Essays on the Human Understanding* (Cambridge: Cambridge University Press, 1996), 2:17 §4: "This definition of 'number' as a multitude of units is appropriate only for whole numbers." Leibniz clarifies this "for number in the broad sense—comprising fractions, irrationals, transcendental numbers and everything which can be found between two whole numbers—is analogous to a line, and does not admit of a minimum any more than the continuum does."

41. Leibniz, "On Freedom," 265–66: "But in proportions the analysis may sometimes be completed, so that we arrive at a common measure which is contained in both terms of the proportion an integral number of times, while sometimes the

analysis can be continued into infinity, as when comparing a rational number with a surd; for instance, the side of a square with the diagonal. Just so, truths are sometimes demonstrable or necessary, and sometimes free and contingent, so that they cannot be reduced to identities as if to a common measure, by any analysis."

42. On the law of curvature [*courbure*] in Leibniz, see "Clarification of the Difficulties which Mr. Bayle Has Found in the New System of the Union of the Soul and Body," in Loemker, *Leibniz.*

43. Leibniz, "On Freedom," §9.

44. On these two types of multiplicity in Leibniz, see M. Serres, *Le Système de Leibniz et ses modèles mathématiques* (Paris, PUF, 1968), 297.

45. Leibniz, "On Freedom," §6.

46. See Gilles Deleuze, *The Fold* (London: Athlone, 1992), where the rapprochement bears on four key points: the same critique of illusions regarding motives, the same conception of the soul, the same conception of inclusion as condition for the free act, and the same description of the free act as expression of the self. See also Worms, *Bergson ou les deux sens de la vie*, 77, which reduces the scope of the rapprochement.

47. *TFW*, 167.

48. Ibid., 169.

49. See Leibniz, "Clarification of the Difficulties," 495–96.

50. *TFW*, 170. See also 135. On the "original bent" [*courbure*] of the soul, see *CE*, 5: "It is with our entire past, including the original bent of our soul, that we desire, will and act." See also *ME*, 45.

51. Leibniz, "On Freedom," §10.

52. *TFW*, 18.

53. See J. Dewey, *Art as Experience* (New York: Perigee, 1980). Dewey describes aesthetic experience precisely as the organic development of a qualitatively unitary experience.

54. *TFW*, 127: "If, then, I question myself carefully on what has just taken place, I perceive that the first four sounds had struck my ear and even affected my consciousness."

55. Ibid., 16–17: "It follows from this analysis that the beautiful is no specific feeling, but that every feeling experienced by us will assume an aesthetic character, provided that it has been suggested, and not caused." Compare the formula

by Prado: "The theory of multiplicities is a kind of transcendental aesthetics. More precisely, it aims to be the definitive version of the transcendental aesthetic, beyond the equivocations of Kantian aesthetics." B. Prado, *Présence et champ transcendental* (Paris: Olms, 2002), 62.

56. See ibid., 7. Sensations are "phenomena which take place on the surface of consciousness, and which are always connected, as we shall see further on, with the perception of a movement or of an external object. But certain states of the soul seem to us, rightly or wrongly, to be self-sufficient, such as deep joy or sorrow, a reflective passion or an aesthetic emotion."

57. Ibid., 158 and 175. Bergson reminds us that *Time and Freewill* consists above all in presenting a "purely negative idea" of the concept of cause, which it is precisely a matter of going beyond.

58. *M*, 325–26.

59. *TSM*, 39: "In the most peaceful emotion there may enter a certain demand for action, which differs from obligation as described above in that it will meet with no resistance, in that it imposes only what has already been acquiesced in, but which none the less resembles obligation in that it does something" [the author quotes Bergson as using the word "creation" in place of "action" above].

60. *CE*, 115.

61. *TFW*, 168.

62. Ibid., 170.

63. Ibid., 172 and also 185: "In truth, the deeper psychic states, those which are translated by free acts, express and sum up the whole of our past history."

64. Ibid., 168–69.

65. [*Esprit* can be translated as "mind" or "spirit"—both translations are adopted here depending on context.]

66. See the example of the mountain in Rousseau in *TSM*, 41: "Rousseau created in connection with them a new and original emotion [. . .] the elementary feelings, akin to sensations, which were directly aroused by the mountains must have been able to harmonise with the new emotion. But Rousseau gathered them together, gave them their places, henceforth as mere harmonics in a sound for which he provided, by a true creation, the principal tone."

67. See *CM*, 28: "We are internal to ourselves, and our personality is what we should know best. Yet such is not the case; our mind is as if it were in a strange land."

68. *TSM*, 236 (our italics).

69. See *MM*, 240: "Our past [. . .] is that which acts no longer but which might act, and will act by inserting itself into a present sensation from which it borrows the vitality."

70. *TSM*, 43. Earlier Bergson gives a precious indication: "Beyond instinct and habit there is no direct action on the will except feeling" (39).

71. Ibid., 253–54.

Intuition and Sympathy

1. *CM*, 135.

2. *CE*, 377. On the relationship between sympathy and aesthetics, refer also to *TFW*, 11–18.

3. *CM*, 169.

4. Ibid. One can see in this extract a sort of allusion to the long period that separates the writing of each of Bergson's books. It is a period in which this relation of sympathy is established. One must constitute a *memory* of the object that equally comprises all the hypotheses, directions of enquiry, errors, tracks that come to cover it over, such that the object becomes a sort of palimpsest of our efforts to constitute it intuitively. The expression "long comradeship" already appears in *TFW* in relation to sympathy (16).

5. We know that Bergson often has recourse to this term—at the outset—to indicate the difference in nature that intuition crosses by its "leap." Hence the access of intuition to matter: "Our eyes are closed to the primordial and fundamental act of perception—that act, constituting pure perception, whereby we place ourselves in the very heart of things" (*MM*, 67). Access to memory is similar: "But the truth is that we shall never reach the past unless we frankly place ourselves within in" (*MM*, 135). It is even the case in the universe of sense or of ideas: "The hearer must place himself at once in the midst of the corresponding ideas" (*MM*, 117).

6. *CM*, 29.

7. Ibid., 21: "Intuition is what attains the spirit, duration, pure change." See also 28: "Quite different is the metaphysics

that we place side by side with science. Granting to science the power of explaining matter by the mere force of intelligence, it reserves mind for itself." Bergson also says that it is an "intimate knowledge of the mind by the mind" or a "reflection of the mind by the mind."

8. See *CE*, 361–32.

9. See *CM*, 93 et seq.

10. *MM*, 235: "No doubt the material universe itself, defined as the totality of images, is a kind of consciousness." See also 37.

11. *CM*.

12. *DS* [*KW*, 208].

13. Ibid.

14. Ibid.

15. *ME*, 6–7: "Reasoning by analogy never gives more than a probability; yet there are numerous cases in which that probability is so high that it amounts to practical certainty. Let us then follow the thread of the analogy and inquire how far consciousness extends, and where it stops." See also *CE*, 255–57. The probabilistic method of "lines of facts" is begun here.

16. *TSM*, 242.

17. Ibid. [translation slightly modified].

18. One finds a perfect illustration of this difference in books 6 and 7 of Plato's *Republic*. The passage on the divided line illustrates the first kind of analogy (structuring of differences in a common resemblance of relations), whereas the allegory of the Cave illustrates the second kind of analogy, of the serial type. The Idea of the Good (absent as dynamic principle of the previous moment) orientates all the terms as a function of its preeminence.

19. Cf. Plato, *Gorgias*, 508a: "Yes, Callicles, wise men claim that partnership and friendship, orderliness, self-control, and justice hold together heaven and earth, and gods and men, and that is why they call this universe a *world order*, my friend, and not an undisciplined world-disorder. I believe that you don't pay attention to these facts, although you are a wise man in these matters. You've failed to notice that proportionate equality has great power among both gods and men, and you suppose that you ought to practice getting the greater share. That's because you neglect geometry." Zeyl translation

in *Plato: Complete Works*, ed. J. M. Cooper (Indianapolis, Ind.: Hackett, 1997).

20. [The author indicates that this passage is in *TSM*. I have been unable to locate it.] See also *CE*, 219: "In a general manner, *measuring* is an entirely human operation."

21. Cf. *TFW*, 119, and *CM*, 160–61.

22. Bergson frequently invokes the "common" as a middle term in his analogies. See, for example, *TFW*, 135. It is the same when it is a matter of criticizing a badly founded analogy. See *TFW*, 120: "Motion itself has nothing in common with this line" [translation modified].

23. See the following important passage in *TSM*: "Except that metaphysics only obtains this direct, internal and certain perception for the movements that it accomplishes itself. Only these can it guarantee are real acts, absolute movements. Already it is not by virtue direct perception, but by virtue of sympathy, for reasons of analogy, that the movements accomplished by other living beings are erected as independent realities. And of the movements of reality in general it can say nothing, if not that there are in all likelihood internal changes that are or are not analogous to efforts, that are accomplished one never knows where and which to our eyes are translated, like our actions, by the reciprocal displacement of bodies in space." The "in all likelihood" is an allusion to the probabilistic nature of analogical reasoning. [On source, see comment for note 125 above.]

24. Some rare but essential passages define memory at the same time as intention and idea. On the memory-idea, see *MM*, 125: "We have said that ideas—pure recollections summoned from the depths of memory—develop into memory images more and more capable of inserting themselves into the motor diagram." On the intention-memory, Bergson evokes "the intention of the memory" (256n76) and "Between the intention, which is what we call the pure memory" (130).

25. On the role of aspiration as a return to the original, see A. Bouaniche, "L'originaire et l'originale, l'unité de l'origine, dans *Les Deux sources de la morale et de la religion*," in *Annales bergsoniennes* (Paris: PUF, 2004), 2:143–70.

26. Deleuze, *Bergsonism*, 44.

27. *CM*, 103. See also 19–20.

28. *M*, 774: "Now, one of the objects of *Creative Evolution*

is to show that the Whole is, on the contrary, of the same nature as the self, and that one grasps it by a more and more complete deepening of oneself."

29. One of the aspects of the celebrated passages on intuition in *MM*, 184: "But there is a last enterprise that might be undertaken. It would be to seek experience at its source, or rather above that decisive *turn* where taking a bias in the direction of our utility, it becomes properly *human* experience."

30. Even personality, considered as duration, is not human. One must distinguish between two uses of the word in Bergson. Sometimes it designates the fact that at each instant, it is our personality in its entirety that inserts itself into the present, although it does so without noticing either intention or spirit. Sometimes, on the contrary, it designates the free acts in which the personality notices itself as a profound appeal, vocation or destiny—that is to say, as "intention."

31. *M*, 485. This passage is not without evoking the transcendental use of the faculties such as Deleuze formulates it in *Difference and Repetition*, 138 et seq. For his part, Bergson talks about "transcendent faculties" (*CM*, 115).

32. *MM*, 185 [translation slightly modified]. See also *CE*, xii: "suppose these other forms of consciousness brought together and amalgamated with the intelligence: would not the result be a consciousness as wide as life? And such a consciousness, turning around suddenly against the push of life which it feels behind, would have a vision of life complete—would it not?—even though the vision were fleeting."

33. *CM*, 168 [translation modified].

34. The intuitive method allows Bergson to "affirm the existence of objects that are inferior and superior to us, although they are internal to us." See on this point Deleuze, *Bergsonism*, 106–7.

35. *TSM*, 103. It was already the error of ancient philosophy, which "suffered itself to be deceived by the purely superficial analogy of duration with extension" *CE*, 210n1.

36. I. Kant, *Critique of Pure Reason*, trans. Norman Kemp Smith (London: Palgrave Macmillan, 2003), 77.

37. On the three syntheses, see Kant, *Critique of Pure Reason*. On the necessity of representing time to oneself so as to know it, see 169: "We cannot obtain for ourselves a representation of time, which is not an object of outer intuition, except under the image of a line, which we draw, and that by

this mode of depicting it alone could we know the singleness of its dimension." It is to this passage and what follows it that the passages in *Time and Freewill* seem to reply directly. See *TFW*, 103, 105–6.

38. *TFW*, 101. Bergson returns frequently to this projection and this badly formed analogy. See 104, 119, 124, 128–31.

39. Ibid., 126.

40. Ibid.: "This proves that our ordinary conception of duration depends on a gradual incursion of space into the domain of pure consciousness." [translation modified]

41. *CM*, 136: "With no other thing can we sympathise intellectually, or if you like, spiritually. But one thing is sure: we sympathise with ourselves."

42. Ibid., 28.

43. See the two affirmations in *MM*, 72: "The sensible qualities of matter would be known in themselves, form within and not from, could we but disengage them from that particular rhythm of duration that characterizes our consciousness." Later: "We are actually placed outside ourselves; we touch the reality of the object in an immediate intuition" (79).

44. *CE*, xiv: "So the present essay does not aim at resolving at once the greatest problems. It simply desires to define the method and to permit a glimpse, on some essential points, of the possibility of its application."

45. Ibid., 30: "The only question is whether the natural systems which we call living beings must be assimilated to the artificial systems that science cuts out within inert matter, or whether they must not rather be compared to that natural system which is the whole of the universe."

46. Deleuze, *Bergsonism*, 105.

47. *CE*, 167: "The instinctive knowledge that one species possesses of another on a certain particular point has its root in the very unity of life, which is, to use the expression of an ancient philosopher, a 'whole sympathetic to itself.'" On the famous example of the Sphex, see 172–73.

48. On instinct as a compressed intuition, see ibid., 181–82.

49. Ibid., 270: "For, with [intuition] we feel ourselves no longer isolated in humanity, humanity no longer seems isolated in the nature that it dominates. [. . .] All the living hold together, and all yield to the same tremendous push."

50. *MM*, 116.

51. Ibid., 210.

52. On this point, see Deleuze, *Bergsonism*, 57. One will find a confirmation of the importance of the question of sense in the fact that Bergson gives an essential privilege to pathologies related to language, such as aphasia.

53. *MM*, 125. Let's recall that there is another version of recognition, which proceeds according to a "sensori-motor" schema and which also calls for a sympathy of a motor order. There is no doubt in this regard that Bergson would have been very interested by the discovery today of what are called "mirror neurons," to the extent that they testify to a properly cerebral sympathetic activity. This discovery calls into question the traditional separation in the brain between sensorial, perceptive and motor functions in the brain , so as to accord to the motor system not just the simple role of execution but one of cognition already present at the level of perception: perceptions thus become "potential actions" which replay actions perceived by the intermediary of these "mirror neurons." The Bergsonian hypothesis, according to which actual perception is already virtual movement, is thereby confirmed. On this point, see G. Rizzolato and C. Sinigaglia, *Les Neurones-miroirs* (Paris: Odile-Jacob, 2008), and cf. *MM*, 13–14.

54. *MM*, 121: "Let us ask [our consciousness] what happens when we listen to the words of another person with the desire to understand them. [. . .] Do we not [. . .] feel that we are adopting a certain disposition, which varies with our interlocutor, with the language he speaks, with the nature of the ideas which he expresses—and varies, above all, with the general movement of his phrase, as though we were choosing the key in which our own intellect is called upon to play?"

55. Ibid., 105.

56. *L*, 41.

57. Deleuze, *Bergsonism*, 80.

58. *DS* [*KW*, 207].

The Attachment to Life

1. It appears a first time in the third chapter of *Matter and Memory* then in *Laughter* (1900), then in the articles on dreams (1901), false recognition (1908), the soul and the body (1908), and the phantasms of the living (1913) [all in *ME*].

2. *MM*, 14.

3. Ibid., 175

4. [The author uses the term *délire* in both its nominal and verbal forms, neither of which is easily translated into English, meaning "delirium," "delusion," "ecstasy," "ravings," and so on. I have rendered the term as "delusion" and "becoming delirious." The reader can refer to J.-J. Lecercle's discussion of this term in Deleuze's work, which the author has in mind here. See J.-J.Lecercle, *Philosophy through the Looking-glass: Language, Nonsense, Desire* (London: Routledge, 1985).]

5. [Passage not located in *TSM* as indicated by author.]

6. One of the last doubts expressed in *The Two Sources* is that "mankind lies groaning, half crushed beneath the weight of its own progress. Men do not sufficiently realise that their future is in their own hands. Theirs is the task of determining whether they want to go on living or not." *TSM*, 317.

7. *MM*, 168.

8. *CM*, 15–117 [quotation slightly modified to agree with grammar of context]. See also *L*, 38.

9. *MM*, 175.

10. Ibid., 174.

11. Ibid., 175.

12. See H. Bergson, *Correspondance* (Paris, PUF, 2002), 579: "I notice in the mind a certain number of 'inhibiting' mechanisms destined incessantly to neutralise or to prevent the morbid phenomena that are virtually there from being produced, and which effectively appear when these mechanisms function badly;—in such a way that diseases of the personality declare themselves from the moment that we no longer have the strength to keep a watch over ourselves."

13. *CE*, 59. On the distraction proper to the normal state, see *ME*, 90.

14. *CE*, 123.

15. Ibid., 123. On the "turning about on the same spot, which the preservation of the species really is," see also *TSM*, 111.

16. Ibid., 205.

17. Ibid., 141: "Deficit, on the contrary, is the *normal* state of the intelligence" (our italics).

18. On the intelligence as a dangerous disturbance, see *TSM*, 129, 138, 207–8.

19. *TSM*, 120–21, 130–31, and 140, respectively.

20. Ibid., 15. This is how we should understand the fine interpretation (doubtless inspired by his reading of Dostoyevsky's *Crime and Punishment*) that Bergson gives of the criminal linked to society "by a thread" which leads to him finally confessing his crime.

21. Ibid., 26.

22. Ibid., 102.

23. Ibid.

24. Ibid., 109. Bergson had earlier affirmed that "religion is what accounts of the storytelling function."

25. Ibid., 76.

26. Ibid., 176: "The truth is that religion, being coextensive with our species, must pertain to our structure."

27. The act of delirium as such is not a vital need, as the myths that free themselves up from belief testify: mythologies, tales, novels.

28. *TSM*, 210.

29. Ibid., 211.

30. Ibid., 158.

31. Ibid., 222.

32. Ibid., 138 [translation modified]. See also 128–29.

33. Ibid., 119.

34. Ibid., 208: "Unrest and story-telling counteract and nullify each other."

35. Ibid., 164.

36. Ibid., 142 and also 152: "Belief, then, means essentially confidence."

37. Ibid., 177.

38. On the circle of the species and the circular conditioning of individual and society (or species), see ibid., 37, 199, 230.

39. See F. Nietzsche's analysis of the case of Socrates in *The Twilight of the Idols, or How to Philosophize with a Hammer* (1889; Harmondsworth: Penguin Classics, 1990), trans. R. J. Hollingdale, §11: "It is self-deception on the part of philosophers and moralists to imagine that by making war on *décadence* they therewith elude *décadence* themselves. This is beyond their powers: what they select as an expedient, as a deliverance, is itself only another expression of *décadence*."

40. *TSM*, 130

41. Cf. *L*, 42

42. *TSM*, 119, 211.

43. On the subject of the mystic, see ibid., 213: "For such a one is more than a man." See also 252.

44. Ibid., 211–12. Cf. 214, where Bergson describes "a quite different attachment to life" and a "transfigured confidence." On the detachment of this new confidence, see what Bergson says about the creative emotion that isn't attached to any object (39–41).

45. *CE*, 124

46. Ibid., 230

47. *TSM*, 223. Bergson invokes a "leap beyond nature" which coincides with the deeper plane of life conceived as "naturing nature."

48. Ibid., 268: "This impetus [*élan*] is thus carried forward through the medium of certain men, each of whom thereby constitutes a species composed of a single individual."

49. On the intensive character of the leap, see ibid., 230, where Bergson invokes a "vibration on one spot."

50. See on this point the confrontation with Janet, ibid., 228.

51. Ibid., 229.

52. *MM*, 235 and 246–47: "Extended matter, regarded as a whole, is like a consciousness where everything balances and compensates and neutralises everything else."

53. Compare, for example, *CE* 355: "A true evolutionism would propose to discover by what *modus vivendi*, gradually obtained, the intelligence has adopted its plan of structure, and matter is mode of subdivision."

54. *MM*, 153 and 155: "These two extreme states, the one of an entirely contemplative memory which apprehends only the singular in its *vision*, the other of a purely motor memory which stamps the note of generality on its *action*, are really separate and are fully visible only in exceptional cases. *In normal life* [our italics] they are interpenetrating, so that each has to abandon some part of its original purity." Bergson comes back to this equilibrium in *TSM*, 228.

55. *TSM*, 229.

56. On the material world as a question posed to motor activity, see *MM*, 45: "As many threads as pass from the periphery to the centre, so many points of space are there able

to make an appeal to my will and to put, so to speak, an elementary question to my motor activity. Every such question is what is termed a perception."

57. *TSM*, 230.

58. It goes without saying that it is not a matter of the voices that mystics claim to hear nor of the hallucinations that accompany them. These words and visions are already mediated by the storytelling function, hence Bergson's "as if." Let's remember that in Bergson, the mystic, considered in his singular essence, is distinct from visions. See ibid., 250: "It would suffice to take mysticism in the unalloyed state, apart from the visions."

59. Ibid., 251: "Let us first note that the mystics ignore what we have called 'false problems'. It may perhaps be objected that they ignore *all* problems, whether real or false, and this is true enough. It is none the less certain that they supply us with an implicit answer to the questions which force themselves upon the attention of philosophers, and that difficulties which should never have perplexed philosophers are implicitly regarded by the mystic as non-existent."

60. See ibid., 253, where Bergson describes a method of composition that "consists in working back from the intellectual and social plane to a point in the soul from which there springs an imperative demand for creation."

61. Ibid., 232.

62. Ibid., 254.

63. On a plane of life that is deeper than the plane of (natured) nature, see *TSM*, 268–69. On the comparison with Spinoza, see ibid., 58.

64. Ibid., 236. It is this intensive economy—expressed by laws of "dichotomy" and "double frenzy"—that Bergson explains in the final chapter, with the hope that the disequilibrium by which humanity is presently seized (total war, extreme industrialization, overpopulation, exhaustion of raw materials) might be counterbalanced by a hitherto repressed inverse tendency. It is not too much to say that the whole of Bergson's philosophy is ordered in terms of these two laws.

65. On "revolt," see *TFW*, 169.

66. On the organic development of creative emotion, see *TFW*, 43–44. On the importance of emotion as generative even of intuition, see Deleuze, *Bergsonism*.

67. *TSM*, 41.

68. *CE*, 237.

69. Deleuze has set out this point from an entirely different point of view. See G. Deleuze, "Bergson's Conception of Difference," in *The Desert Island and Other Texts* (New York: Semiotext(e), 2004), 50: "That which differs in nature is in the end that which differs in nature *from itself*, consequently, that from which it differs is only its lowest *degree*. [. . .] When the difference of nature between two things has become one of the two things, the other of the two is only the *last* degree of the first."

70. *CE*, 238: "Life [. . .] is like an effort to raise the weight which falls. True, it succeeds only in retarding the fall. But at least it can give us an idea of what the raising of the weight was." One might think here of A. Giacometti's remarks in *Alberto Giacometti* (Paris: Musee de l'Art Moderne de la ville de Paris, 1991), 415: "I know that it is entirely impossible for me to model, paint, or sketch a head, for example, as it see it and yet it is the only think that I try to do. Everything that I can do will only ever be a pale image of what I see, and my success will always be below my failure, or perhaps always equal to my failure." But it is perhaps Beckett who best summarizes this double tendency by the double imperatives of *Worstward Ho* (New York: Grove, 1984): Try again, fail again, fail better.

71. *TSM*, 232.

72. Ibid.

73. Ibid., 254. On the difference between the mystic and the artist, cf. A. Bouaniche, "Bergson et Merleau-Ponty: Le mystique et l'artiste dans le moment de la Seconde Guerre mondiale," in *La Mystique face aux guerres mondiales*, ed. D. de Courcelles and G. Waterlot (Paris: PUF, 2010).

74. Ibid.

75. On the passage from the world to the universe, see ibid., 258–59.

After Man

1. This is one of the terms that recurs most frequently in Bergson to characterize the intelligence's mode of functioning. Thus there is the "circle of necessity" of determinist thinking, the circle of nominalism and conceptualism, the "circle of the given," and even the circle of laughter.

2. On the critique of spiritualism see *CE*, 259 et seq.

3. *CM*, 21: "Pure change, real duration, is a thing spiritual or impregnated with spirituality. Intuition is what attains the spirit, duration, pure change."

4. Ibid., 103–4 [translation slightly modified].

5. *CE*, 192. See also *M*, 774: "It seems to me, on the contrary, that for everyone, a knowledge that grasps its object from the *inside*, that apperceives it such as it would apperceive itself if its apperception and its existence were one and the same thing, is an absolute knowledge, a knowledge of the absolute. It is not knowledge of *all* of reality, doubtless; but relative knowledge is one, limited knowledge another."

6. For example, *CE*, 258: "Intuition is there, however, but vague and above all discontinuous. It is a lamp almost extinguished, which only glimmers now and then, for a few moments at most."

7. *MM*, 208.

8. *CE*, 260: "The movement of the stream is distinct from the river bed, although it must adopt its winding course."

9. Compare, for example, the opposition set out by Riquier between the verbs "to found" [*fonder*] and "to merge/cast/found" [*fondre*] in *Archéologie de Bergson*, 25 et seq.

David Lapoujade teaches philosophy at Paris-I Panthéon-Sorbonne.

Andrew Goffey is associate professor in critical theory and cultural studies at the University of Nottingham.